2017 PM360 ELITE Award Winner

*Recognized as one of the 100 most influential people
in the healthcare industry.*

Mike Veny

MIKE VENY

TRANSFORMING STIGMA™

HOW TO BECOME A
MENTAL WELLNESS
SUPERHERO

Transforming Stigma by Mike Veny

Published by Mike Veny, Inc.

PO Box 150252

Kew Gardens, NY 11415-0252

www.TransformingStigma.com

© 2018 Mike Veny, Inc.

team@mikeveny.com

The Transforming Stigma™ phrase is a trademark of Mike Veny, Inc.

First edition.

ISBN-13: 978-0-692-04862-7

DEDICATION

This book is dedicated to Cheryl Williams. Thank you for believing in me and encouraging me to share the story of my mental health challenges. You have had such a positive impact on so many lives and I am honored to know you.

TRIGGER WARNING: This book discusses violence, self-harm, and suicide.

WARNING – DISCLAIMER: The purpose of this book is to educate and entertain. The author and/or publisher shall have neither liability nor responsibility to anyone with respect to any loss or damaged caused, directly or indirectly, by the information contained in this book. The author is not a mental health professional. If you need medical help, please consult a doctor. **If you are in an emergency, please call 911.**

NOTE: Throughout this book the author uses the term "mental health challenges" in places where one might typically say "mental health issues" or "mental illness". He made the decision to do this because "mental health challenges" feels less stigmatizing to him.

ONE MORE NOTE: Some names and identifying details have been changed to protect the privacy of individuals.

I hope you find what I've written to be helpful. If you have any feedback or questions, here's how to contact me:

Mike Veny
PO Box 150252
Kew Gardens, New York 11415-0252
USA

www.TransformingStigma.com

If you enjoy this book, please leave a positive review on Amazon.com.

CONTENTS

INTRODUCTION

The number of people struggling with mental health challenges is growing by the day. The World Health Organization estimates that 300 million people worldwide are affected by depression,[1] the most common mental health issue, right now. In many cases, depression is a catalyst that leads people to think about or attempt suicide.

According to the American Foundation for Suicide Prevention, suicide is the 10th leading cause of death in the United States. Approximately 44,000 Americans die by suicide each year. Out of every 25 people who attempt suicide, one will succeed. Along with these staggering emotional statistics, the economy is also affected as suicide costs $50 billion annually.[2]

Besides depression, mental health challenges can also include bipolar affective disorder, schizophrenia, dementia, developmental disorders including autism, and the list goes on and on.

Left untreated, these challenges affect other areas of your life. They will have a negative impact on your physical health, work, education, housing, ability to drive, family, holidays, spirituality, and more.

The National Bureau of Economic Research says there's "[a] defi-

---

1 "Depression." World Health Organization. Accessed December 2017. http://www.who.int/mediacentre/factsheets/fs369/en/.

2 "Suicide Statistics — AFSP." American Foundation for Suicide Prevention. Accessed December 2017. https://afsp.org/about-suicide/suicide-statistics/.

nite connection between mental illness and the use of addictive substances." In fact, people living with these challenges are responsible for the consumption of 38% of alcohol, 44% of cocaine, and 40% of cigarettes. Any of these combinations or any number of other combinations can each develop with their own unique causes and symptoms.[3]

Substance abuse affects one's finances. But even if someone isn't using, they can still experience a dent in their finances because of mental challenges. In 2007, the World Health Organization released a report titled Breaking The Vicious Cycle Between Mental Ill-Health and Poverty. The report highlightings the correlation between mental health challenges and poverty.

For example, people living in poverty who are hungry and in debt are more likely to struggle with mental health challenges. People who struggle with mental health challenges also have a much more difficult time finding housing, which increases the chances that they will become homeless.

The report concluded that the link between mental health challenges and poverty was cyclical. Poverty increases the risk of mental health challenges, and people with mental health challenges are at risk for descending into poverty.[4]

With such a profound impact on our economy, you would think we would put your time and money into fixing the issue. However, on average, only 2% of a country's budget is dedicated to men-

3 Cuellar, Alison Evans, Sara Markowitz, and Anne M. Libby. "The Relationships between Mental Health and Substance Abuse Treatment and Juvenile Crime." NBER. Accessed December 2017. http://www.nber.org/papers/w9952.

4 Breaking The Vicious Cycle Between Mental Ill-Health and Poverty. Report. September 4, 2017. Accessed December 2017. http://www.who.int/mental_health/policy/development/1_Breakingviciouscycle_Infosheet.pdf

tal health treatment and 31% of countries have no mental health treatment budget at all. 76% to 85% of people with serious mental health challenges do not receive treatment in developing countries.

Without this treatment, people suffer even more. When mental health treatment options are made available, they are better able to find work, take better care of their overall health, and they are empowered to rise out of poverty. Available treatment also has been shown to help combat other diseases such as HIV/AIDS, malaria, and others.

Several countries have taken huge steps forward to address mental health challenges. One of the them is the United Kingdom. An organization called Heads Together, backed by Prince William, Kate Middleton, and Prince Harry, has initiated a campaign to transform stigma in the UK.

The campaign uses video and social media to transform the negative attitudes and perceptions of mental health in the UK. This has led to an increase in conversations about mental health around the country.

Superheroes who have been vocal in this campaign include Ruby Wax; Alistair Campbell; Mark Austin; Freddie Flintoff; and Steve Manderson, better known as Professor Green. They have leveraged their popularity as celebrities and attracted a host of other celebrities to help spread this project, impacting their fans, their country, and others around the world.

We may not have access to an audience as large as a famous musician or world-renowned actor, but we all have interactions with people we can help. In my work as a mental health speaker, school administrators often hire me to speak to their students—to spread hope and raise understanding and awareness of mental health challenges. These calls, far too often, are the result of a tragic incident or the overall increase in the number of deaths by suicide in a school or district.

In my opinion, this is one of the most important issues of our time, and if you are not being affected with mental health challenges, I guarantee that you know someone who is. The statistics keep rising and pretty soon this will become a worldwide epidemic if we don't do something about it.

This book provides the framework for a solution to help yourself, your loved ones, and our society. In fact, the solution is very simple. It involves a paradigm shift in how you view the subject of mental health.

This solution also involves developing new habits. Most importantly, it involves taking an honest, a brutally honest, look at yourself.

To be transparent with you, I'm not a mental health professional. I don't have any credentials recognized by any educational institution that give me a foundation for expertise on this subject. However, I am a person who has been living with mental health challenges for my entire life.

My own life experiences and my work as a mental health speaker have empowered me to approach this subject from a new perspective. For me, it's been a lifetime of emotional pain and unhealthy relationships since mental health challenges and people issues go hand in hand.

This is why I have made it my company's mission to *Help people heal emotional pain and discover meaning through simple ideas that empower wellness and healthy relationships.*

Knowing that other people are struggling with these challenges makes me angry and frustrated because I know what it feels like to struggle with my challenges each day, and the whole subject seems like a never ending mystery.

I am deeply saddened when I learn that someone has died by suicide. I know what it feels like to have no hope and think there's no other solution. I've also known too many people who died by suicide.

For the past seven years, I have been a professional mental health speaker. I didn't choose this profession by choice. It simply fell into my lap, and I surrendered to do it.

Through speaking at events, I have met people who struggled like me. Some seemed to have it easier and others seemed to have it much worse. I've listened to many stories and learned lots of lessons as I have worked hard to make my presentations more thorough, impactful, and empowering for my audiences.

If you read this book thoroughly and are open to my suggestions, you will become mentally healthier. You will also gain new tools to help people in your life who are struggling.

Your efforts are critical to helping our entire society become mentally healthier. You will be part of the solution to reduce (and hopefully eliminate) suicide, which in turn will reduce crime and violence while making our economy more productive.

"He was engaging and has a unique gift of including his audience in a way that promotes healing through a shared experience. I believe he would be an asset to any community seeking to energize, focus and enlighten its members on a common goal. For our occasion it was mental illness however I believe his candor, humor and transparency are applicable in a variety of corporate and community settings."
Sophie F. Clark, Executive Director, NAMI DC

"With humor, optimism, and quality interventions, he provided us with useful strategies to employ in our classrooms. Mike's gift for working with children with special needs is apparent to all who had the privilege of listening to his message."

Cheryl Rosenfeld, Director of Westcop Therapeutic Nursery and Head Start

"He was so inspiring and real. He told it like it was and left us with ideas of how to work on the stigma. He not only shared information, but solutions."

Event Attendee

"We had 602 participants from many of the mental health and substance abuse groups around the state of Arkansas. Our participants have to do more work with less money every year. What keeps them in the profession is caring for their clients and helping them have better lives. Your talk helped them see that their work has meaning and that their efforts count. There is always room for improvement in mental health counseling, but you helped them see this in a gifted way."

Charlotte Besch, Program Manager, MidSOUTH/UALR School of Social Work

"Students were better able to understand that depression is an illness that can be treated."

Jesicah Rolapp, Principal, Los Angeles Leadership Academy

Here's my promise to you: I promise that if you blindly trust me, you will gain some simple insights and practical tools that you can apply within 24 hours after finishing this book.

Ultimately, you will live a happier life and make this a better world.

Superheroes aren't just fictional characters from comic books, television shows, and movies. They exist among us in everyday life.

Superheroes can teach you so much about yourself. In this chapter, you will learn why it's important to become a mental wellness superhero.

CHAPTER 1

SUPERHEROES

The purpose of this book is to turn you into a superhero. If asked to draw yourself as a superhero, what would you look like? What would your name be?

What superpowers would you have? What one weakness would you hide from your enemies like your life depends on it? Picture this superhero in your mind.

What if, instead of picturing this superhero in your mind, someone drew you as a superhero, based on their perception of you? This picture would show a completely different superhero than the one you pictured. If you asked 100 people to do the same exercise, it's very possible you would get 100 different superheroes, all drawn to represent you—a single person.

Although our portrayal of ourselves and how others see us is different, there will be some similarities. These are the same traits that connect us with others, which is explained by homophily—the tendency of individuals to associate and bond with others who are similar. Even if vastly different on the surface, there are many traits and characteristics that connect us to the people we love, celebrities, and even fictional superheroes.

And make no mistake about it—how others perceive us has a huge impact on how they view, treat, and talk about us. Just as you might feel scared of someone approaching you with a physical disfigurement at night while you're walking home alone, people with mental health challenges are often viewed as dangerous individuals who pose a threat to others.

Thus, those with mental health challenges need a superhero. Every superhero, including you, needs an injustice to fight, and the perception of mental health in our society is an injustice worth fighting against.

The negative perception of mental health damages lives and limits the potential of extraordinary people. Because there's an "illness" attached to us, we're treated differently. We even treat ourselves adversely.

While treatment and education in the mental health space is increasing and gaining more funding, there is a miracle-like change that is still needed. By reading this book and taking action on the information and challenges presented, you can lead the charge to transform the stigma, which as you'll learn, is a fight worth fighting and not something requiring you to have superhuman abilities.

As you learn to understand mental health challenges in a way you can relate to, you will learn to transform the stigma. If you think you can't relate, just look at the stories of *Alice and Wonderland* and *The Hulk* as they are now examples used in the mental health field.

The Hulk, also known as The Incredible Hulk, represents both a human and a monster. He's big, muscular, green, and always angry. The angrier he becomes, the more his rage and physical physique grows.

The Hulk is the alter ego of Bruce Banner, a humble physicist who appears to be an introvert. Despite appearing calm and reserved, he transforms into The Hulk when emotionally triggered and causes physical damage to anything and everything that gets in his way.

As the popularity of The Hulk grew in comic books, the demand to see him in action inspired a TV series. Beginning in 1978, the one-hour weekly show featured actor Bill Bixby as Bruce Banner and bodybuilder Lou Ferrigno as The Hulk. Families across the country could now see the comic book-based character in action.

Forty years later, the Hulk is as popular as ever. Over the past few decades, The Hulk has been featured in four full-length feature films: *Hulk* (2003), *The Incredible Hulk* (2008), *The Avengers* (2012), and *Avengers: Age of Ultron* (2015), and appeared in numerous animated films and series.

The Hulk connects with viewers unlike any other superhero. People connect with both the mild-mannered physicist who is an intelligent introvert, and the angry and volatile Hulk he becomes.

Have you ever felt like the intelligent introvert? How about the raging Hulk ready to wreak havoc at any moment? Our ability to connect with both characters goes far beyond entertainment—it's a reflection of ourselves.

We all experience ebbs and flows of thoughts and behaviors that can be hurtful to others, like in the case of The Hulk. These thoughts and behaviors can also be harmful to ourselves, even if the drama plays out solely in our minds.

A little over two decades before the introduction of *The Incredible Hulk*, Walt Disney Productions produced a film called *Alice in Wonderland* (1951). Based on the 1865 novel *Alice's Adventures in Wonderland* by author Lewis Carroll, the film brings to life the story of a girl named Alice who falls through a rabbit hole into a strange world.

Alice encounters a talking doorknob, the Mad Hatter, and the tyrannical Queen of Hearts who beheads her enemies. At the end of the story, Alice realizes that her journey into Wonderland and fall down the rabbit hole was in her mind and not real in a physical sense. Although none of the outlandish events that happened in her mind were real to anyone else, they were very real to her.

Like Alice, many people go down rabbit holes in their minds, whether pleasant daydreams or truly terrifying situations. They become entangled in strange worlds that seem and feel completely real to them. Alice awakes from her dream to a seemingly normal world, however, the memories and experiences stay with her long after they are over.

Although both characters, The Hulk and Alice, are fictional and completely unique, we feel a connection to both. It's not because we also could envision a murderous queen or a talking doorknob, or because we are capable of destroying things when we're angry, but because we all use our imagination, have moments of anger, and can get trapped in our own minds.

While comparing people to animated and fictional characters may not fully address the complexity of mental health challenges, the relatability of the characters helps us see what these disorders are capable of while understanding that they affect everyone in one way or another. Like those who are living with mental health challenges, The Hulk and Alice have positive traits and characteristics along with dark times and obstacles that when left unaddressed, can have real, tragic consequences.

On December 14th, 2012, Adam Lanza walked into Sandy Hook Elementary School. Armed with hundreds of rounds of ammunition, Lanza opened fire on innocent children and school staff, killing twenty school children and six staff members.

At the time of this writing, the Sandy Hook tragedy is the deadliest mass shooting at a high school or grade school in the history of the United States. It's also the third-deadliest shooting by a single person in the country's history, after the 2016 shooting inside the Pulse nightclub in Orlando and the 2007 Virginia Tech University shooting that took the lives of thirty-two people and injured many others.

Shortly before entering Sandy Hook Elementary School, Adam Lanza shot and killed his mother, Nancy Lanza. According to a variety of news reports, Nancy Lanza was a passionate gun enthusiast who stored her guns unprotected, allowing access to anyone in the home, including Adam.

The event was a catalyst for intensifying the never-ending gun control debate in the US. As the media highlighted passionate arguments from both sides, another debate began to emerge. Regardless of whether or not Adam Lanza's easy access to the guns contributed to the problem, most people agree that he intended to inflict harm. His harmful intentions brought the status of his mental health into question.

According to an article by Alison Leigh Cowan, "Medical experts at Yale University had called for drastic measures to help Adam Lanza in the years before he shot and killed 26 people at Sandy Hook Elementary School in Newtown, Conn., but those calls allegedly 'went largely unheeded' by his mother."[5]

What could've stopped Adam or helped him get the help he needed is debatable, but the truth is there were signs others ignored. He was someone in need of help, and unfortunately, took his personal pain and struggles and used them to inflict pain on others. Let me be clear: **I don't believe that this tragic shooting happened because of his mental health challenges, but it's obvious that more could've been done to help Lanza.**

Those who intend to inflict harm on others, for whatever reason, will always find a way to do so. Preventing these heinous acts won't come from ridding the country or world of every gun, knife, nuclear weapon, or rock. Tapping into the root of the problem is where we need to start. Hulk's and Alice's exist everywhere, including within ourselves, and the people we love. As we continue to learn more about those who are struggling, and get them the help that they need, we will be better able to empower every person to live the best life possible.

It's up to us to be and empower others to become mental health superheroes. This may not be the type of superhero you pictured for yourself, but this will give you real opportunity to save lives and change the world.

There are tens of millions of people in the U.S. alone who need your help. You may not be able to hear their call for help right now, but they are in need. Our is hungry for superheroes who will champion mental health and rid the universe of the stigma. Are you one of those superheroes?

---

5 Alison L. Cowan,. "Adam Lanza's Mental Problems 'Completely Untreated' Before Newtown Shootings." New York Times, November 22, 2014. Accessed December 2017. https://www.nytimes.com/2014/11/22/nyregion/before-newtown-shootings-adam-lanzas-mental-problems-completely-untreated-report-says.html.

As someone with this book in their hands who has read through this chapter, I truly believe you are this superhero.

Are you ready to earn your tight-fitting spandex tights, cape, and new superpower?

If so, the first step in your superhero training, which is designed to help you transform the stigma surrounding mental health, is to blindly trust me. I need you to take a leap of faith into the pages that follow as we take this journey together. Agreed?

Up, up, and away we go!

PART 1

MY STORY

In this chapter, you'll learn about my earliest childhood memories through my fourth grade year of school. You'll also learn about my earliest memories of living with mental health challenges.

When people use the phrase 'mental health', they are referring to thoughts, feelings, and behavior. You can't see someone's thoughts or feel their feelings, but you can observe their behavior.

CHAPTER 2

THE BED

Superheroes have always played an important role in my life. They are a part of my earliest memories. As a child, the heroes I looked up to didn't always wear tight pants or have superpowers; they represented comfort, inspiration, and an escape from tough times.

I remember sitting on the floor of my parents' bedroom as a three-year-old and staring in wonder.

I wasn't looking at my mom or dad, but the evening news with Tom Brokaw, and then the friendly and furry creatures on Sesame Street. My mom would sit me in front of the glowing, warm piece of technology to keep me entertained for hours at a time. These happy memories included bouncing up and down to drum beats and being completely caught up in each song during music interludes on Sesame Street.

Having characters on television serve as my role models played a significant role in my development as a child. Through these role models, I gained insight into life outside of my home, or at least how it was portrayed on television. I also learned how people communicated with each other, and how I should treat others.

What I didn't learn was how to process my own feelings and work through confusing emotions. Televisions are great for entertainment, but lacking in in-depth communication.

Television presented a fantasy land for me—a place where I could escape from my life. Life seemed better on television than it played out in real life.

Despite putting me in front of the television for long stretches, I was loved intensely by my mother, and I knew it. She would constantly show me love and enthusiastic praise, spend time with me, and put me first, or at least I thought. But at times, something would change in an instant.

It seemed as though a switch inside my mother would flip, and the mom who showed me extraordinary love would almost instantly be replaced by someone who was completely unavailable, selfish and unpredictable. This happened frequently although I never knew when it was coming.

This back and forth—showing me love one second and not wanting anything to do with me the next—felt worse than constant neglect because I had no idea what to expect or what I had done to cause this change in her. I knew something was wrong, and I thought it was me, but I couldn't process my emotions or the situation.

To give me something to do other than stare at the television, my parents bought art supplies and encouraged me to express myself artistically. "You're such a creative and talented little artist," my mother said looking down at me as I was drawing. "You're going to be a great artist someday."

After she said that, I felt an immediate boost in my confidence, and for the first time, pressure. I wanted my mother to be happy with me, and if she thought I was going to be a great artist, I needed to become that. I began concentrating on my art to impress her.

I watched my mother closely as she did chores and got ready for the day. My mother was a beautiful, lean, African-American 5'5" woman. However, she had very light skin, brunette hair, and brown eyes. Because of her skin tone and the texture of her hair, people often thought she was Caucasian or Latino. She put a lot of time and care into her appearance, and she never left the house without putting on her lipstick.

One day, I decided to draw a picture of her bright red lipstick. I picked out the colors I needed, prepared my approach, and laid out my paper canvas. I meticulously envisioned the container and the shape of the cap.

As I began drawing my picture of her lipstick, I felt my stomach drop. Something wasn't right with my drawing. I went to get her lipstick to compare the two.

Putting them side-by-side, nothing matched. On my drawing, the lines were uneven, the size of the cap was disproportionate to the size of the base of the lipstick, and the colors were off. For the first time I can remember, I felt like I had failed.

The disappointment and anger I felt went deeper than my dissatisfaction with the drawing—I felt like a complete failure and a terrible artist. My work belonged in a garbage can, not a museum, and I knew that Mommy wasn't going to be happy with me. I feared that she would lose faith in my artistic ability, and ultimately, lose faith in me.

My mother was not easily angered, but she was hard to please, and I felt the weight of the world on my shoulders trying to gain her approval. Even when I felt like I had earned her approval, it was only a matter of time before things seemed to change in an instant, and I started to once again feel like I had failed and caused the constant shifts in her mood.

Despite all of this, I still considered this to be a very happy time in my life. I got love and attention from my parents, had free access to the television, and had everything I could've asked for. And then Jason came.

Leading up to the birth of my brother, Jason, everyone was excited, except me. I was a happy three-year-old who didn't understand why we needed another person in the family. Wasn't I enough for my parents?

The affection and attention that shifted from me to Jason when he was born hurt me deeply. I cycled through feelings of anger, hurt, and anxiety, which resulted in me misbehaving. I stopped listening to instructions, hit my little brother, which I still regret, and remember yelling at the top of my lungs on many occasions for little to no reason.

In responses to my behavior, my father would often yell at me and tell me that I was jealous. That made me feel worse.

The reality was that I felt like I received less love and care when my brother entered the picture, and I began to feel left out. This change shifted my feelings and behavior.

While I knew things like hitting my brother and screaming at my parents were wrong, I kept doing it, and I didn't understand why. Getting yelled at or punished, which I hated, didn't fix why I was mad or what caused me to act out.

When I misbehaved, my parents never took the time to explain to me why a particular behavior was wrong. I just got yelled at, and it made me feel horrible.

And it only temporarily fixed my behavior since I stopped only out of fear of humiliation. I felt ashamed, scared, and unsafe, especially when my father yelled at me.

My father was the authority figure in the family. He was a 5'9" African American man with an average build, a bushy mustache, thick glasses, and a balding head. He worked full-time as a customs broker in Inwood, New York, while my mother stayed home to take care of my brother and me at our home in Hempstead, New York.

A few years after Jason was born, another difficult shift took place—I began attending school.

Once I began kindergarten in Uniondale, our local school district, I had my first real social experience with kids my own age on a regular basis.

It was comforting to know that most of the people were the same color as me, black or brown. That felt very familiar and comfortable for some reason.

In first grade, I began to feel self-conscious. This included feeling embarrassed when my teacher asked me to respond to a question in class, or when I was called on.

My first grade teacher was attractive, and I had a crush on her. Once I found out that she was changing her last name and getting married, I remember feeling a sense of loss or anger.

After I learned that my crush was getting married, I came home from school and intentionally didn't tell my parents about a homework assignment my teacher had given me.

"The dog ate it," I told the teacher when she asked where my homework was the following day. Obviously, my dog didn't eat my homework. We didn't even have a dog.

I didn't want to do my homework, didn't do it, and decided to intentionally lie to see what would happen. Part of me felt bad for lying, but I also felt a sense of power and achievement.

The teacher told my parents about this and other ways I was acting out at school. Understandably, my parents were frustrated with me, and I could sense their anxiety around how to deal with my behavior problems.

So what do you do with a kid who tries to control situations and take advantage of teachers? You turn to God. My parents decided to send me to Catholic school.

Religion was very confusing to me. I was baptized Lutheran, my dad was Baptist, my mother was Catholic, and my grandmother was Episcopalian. Prior to kindergarten, I attended a Lutheran school for preschool when I was three years old and loved it. Back then, I played and painted all day.

In second grade, my parents put my brother and I in Catholic school, which I found confusing to an extent because I was being raised Lutheran. I knew that the Catholic religion was very different. I often questioned my faith.

Was the Catholic religion "The right religion" and my religion was "Wrong"? Why were they different? Why did my mom push Catholic school over me going to another Lutheran school?

My mom was passionate about Catholic school because she had attended a Catholic school herself, and felt that it was the ultimate form of education because of the discipline that she gained. Mommy was always right, right?

In the Uniondale School District, where I attended school prior to this, the majority of classmates looked just like me. However, the Catholic school where my parents enrolled us in, Corpus Christi School in Mineola, New York, was much different. Most of the students there were of Eastern European descent. They were from a different world than me.

They all knew each other, had playdates, and were on the same sports teams. I was the "new kid" and felt like an outsider. I tried my best to make friends and not cause any trouble.

One evening, my parents took Jason and I along to go shopping at the Roosevelt Field Mall. As they stood in line at the bookstore, I asked if I could go look at magazines, and they said yes.

As I began browsing the colorful magazine covers, a Playboy magazine caught my eye. Even at such a young age, I knew exactly what it was. It was also within my reach.

I really wanted to see what was inside it. I'd never really seen a naked woman before. So being very aware of my surroundings, I took the magazine, walked into another aisle, dropped it, went to go pick it up, and slid it under my jacket sleeve.

With the Playboy magazine in my jacket sleeve, we drove home. I knew that my mother would not check my jacket that evening. When we got home, I put it in my backpack for school the following day.

On the morning bus ride, I showed everybody my Playboy Magazine, and all the boys were looking at it. I kept it in my bag throughout the school day, but knew that my mother would check my bag when I got home from school.

Before leaving school, I went into the boys' bathroom and threw the Playboy Magazine out the window. It landed somewhere in a stairwell near the back parking lot of the school.

Stealing an adult magazine from a bookstore and bringing it to school was the most delinquent behavior I had during that time. Somehow, I made it through the second and third grade without any other behavior challenges. But this wouldn't last long.

My 4th grade year, when I was 9 going on 10, was a defining year of my life. It began with hope and ended lower than what I could've possibly comprehended as a 9 year old.

One day, earlier in the school year, the music instructor brought in instruments to raise interest in joining the school's band. I wasn't paying much attention to the demonstration until the crisp sound of a snare drum shot through my ears. I couldn't turn away.

It was as if the sound was controlling me in an exciting and freeing way. I knew, at that moment, I was meant to play the drums.

"No," my father said as I begged him to let me play the drums. "Because I said so," was the best reason he could give. He took the only thing I wanted to do at the time away from me because he wanted to.

But my disappointment didn't end there, it continued into the classroom. "Wipe that smile off your face," said Sister Pat, considered the meanest, strictest teacher, as I sat at my desk.

The other kids feared her and made sure not to get on her bad side, but I wasn't afraid. I was sitting in the back of the classroom one day with a big grin on my face. Sister Pat didn't like the fact that I was smiling and told me to "wipe the smile off of my face".

"No," I replied.

"Oooooooooooo," several classmates said under their breath in unison anxiously awaiting what Sister Pat was going to do. In an instant, she was now standing next to my desk, and we were in the middle of a heated exchange.

I felt her cold, wrinkly hand touch my right arm. "I'm taking you out to the office." I replied by throwing a punch while saying, "don't touch me!"

"You're the devil," she said as she reached in her pocket for her bottle of holy water. She opened the bottle and proceeded to throw some on me. After I recommended she use the rest of the holy water on her wrinkles, she took me down to the principal's office, and I spent the next week at home away from school.

It was clear that catholic school—where authority figures used an aggressive style of discipline was not a good fit for me. I was expelled from Catholic school in the fall of my fourth grade year and needed to figure out what I school I would go to next.

My parents had a new idea—public school. This wasn't just any public school, but one where my Uncle Billy was the principal. If anyone could keep me in line, they figured that he could.

After several weeks in my new school, my class attended a school band concert during the school day. Listening to the band perform was mesmerizing. Just like the snare drum captured my attention at the Catholic school, hearing the bass and snare drum did something to me that's still hard to explain. I could feel each beat of the drum go through my entire body. This gave me a sense of raw power and happy feelings.

When I got home from the school that day, fearing the worst but hoping for the best, I asked my dad if I could play the drums one more time. Maybe I wore him down or he realized that learning to play an instrument would be good for me because he actually said yes! I was more excited than I had ever been up to that point in my life.

That excitement very quickly turned to disappointment when I learned that there were no spots for additional drummers in the band. Instead, they handed me a stupid trombone.

Like my excitement to play the drums in the school band, my parents hope and excitement that this school would be a fit for me was quickly dashed. After several fights, outbursts, and a desk mysteriously jumping out of my hands and flying in the direction of a teacher, I was "asked" to leave the school.

By January, I had been expelled from two schools because of my behavior. Something didn't seem right about this.

For the remainder of the year, a tutor came to our home each day. The tutor rarely made eye contact with me, like she was afraid. The minute each session was over, she would rush out of our house like someone was chasing her.

Based on the thoughts in my head, it was hard enough to think I was "normal;"however, when other people confirmed these thoughts, like the tutor with the way she acted around me, I was forced to deal with the realization that I was different, and possibly "crazy."

Oftentimes, when I was watching TV or during dinner, I would hear my parents throw around words like "suspended," "expelled," "psychologist," "psychiatrist," and "special education."

Those words hurt. They didn't hurt because I fully understood what they meant; they hurt because of the tone in which they were said.

My parents said them with frustration because something was wrong with me. I knew it, and so did they.

I managed to get through the rest of the school year being tutored from home without any problems outside of the tutor being

terrified to work with me. Looking back, I think I was more successful with a tutor in my home because the majority of the distractions
that could have triggered me were out of the picture.

There were no other students, formal classes, teachers, lockers,
announcements, or other things to manage or worry about. Getting through the rest of the year with this tutor was an accomplishment of sorts, but none of the problems experienced at previous
schools were resolved. This was just the calm before the storm.

That storm began innocently enough. It was the summer of 1989,
and the movie *Batman*, starring Michael Keaton and Jack Nicholson
had just been released. As a family, we went to see the movie, and I
was extremely excited to see it.

I always felt a strong connection with the Batman character. Batman had good intentions, but a dark demeanor that I could relate
with. That darkness always got darker when Batman dealt with a
particularly dark villain — like The Joker.

At the end of the film, The Joker, played by Jack Nicholson, is
pulled down from a ladder attached to a helicopter by a grappling
hook. The metal wire attached to the grappling hook is wrapped
around a gargoyle on the roof of a building on one end, compliments of Batman, and the other end is around The Joker's leg.

As the helicopter rises, pressure is put on both the gargoyle and
The Joker's leg. The gargoyle, under the pressure of the solid metal wire, breaks from the roof of the building and takes the Joker
along with it down to the concrete below. The Joker is plunged to
his death.

Later on that day, I plummeted, similar to The Joker. To be clear, I
didn't fall off the roof of a building, but I began to feel some intense
anger for reasons I didn't understand.

This anger stretched me like the wire between the gargoyle and The Joker. I reached a point where there wasn't a safe way down. I felt like there was nowhere to go emotionally.

I exploded.

I began by moving my solid wood dresser to barricade my bedroom door. The sound of wood scraping on the floor alerted my mom. "Hey, what are you doing that's making so much noise?" my mother said. I didn't answer, and no one came upstairs to see what I was doing, so I turned it up a notch.

After my dresser was firmly in front of my door, I looked around my room for things worth throwing. I tossed anything I could against the wall. As my mom's suspicions grew, she knew she needed to get involved.

After several attempts to open my door, she made a peace offering -— buying me a meal from Taco Bell. Taco Bell did sound good, but I wasn't going to give up that easily. To answer her offer, I opened my bedroom window and started throwing the additional items outside.

Nearby neighbors stepped out of their homes and looked up at me as I yelled, swore, and threw everything in my room onto the ground below. The stunned looks on their faces gave me satisfaction.

I felt superhuman and wasn't going to stop, no matter what the consequences were. I knew that I was just a 9-year-old little kid, but emotionally, I felt invincible.

Like any superhero gone bad, the police were called to minimize the damage. Minutes later I was taken to Nassau County Medical Center, a hospital nearby.

My dad and I sat for hours in the hospital's emergency room.

When my name was called, I went into a small room with the psychiatrist. The psychiatrist, a woman in her 40's or 50's, asked me a series of questions.

If I answered truthfully, I knew that I would be admitted into the hospital. I thought about lying, but I was too exhausted to lie, and on some level, I wanted to get the help I knew I needed.

I decided to answer her truthfully, and for the first time, became a patient in a mental hospital. My behavior earned every bit of the experience—from the deep dark green walls to the hospital gown I was given to wear at Nassau County Medical Center.

With the snap of my fingers, I transitioned from having a bedroom at home that was now covered in broken things, to a cold, bare room with white sheets, blankets, a few shelves, and a window. I knew this was not an overnight stay; I was here for awhile and needed to make a change.

I felt like I was in prison on the outside and the inside. The hospital faced Hempstead Turnpike, but all I could see were lights and barbed wire fences from my room.

At night, I used to look out the hospital windows, which were locked shut. I tried many times to open them in hopes of escaping this nightmare.

I told my parents that I didn't want to discuss my hospitalization with anyone, in part because I was ashamed and also because it just wasn't something you shared. My family also wanted to keep this embarrassing situation a secret.

I didn't want the world to know about it, but even worse than fearing that this secret would get out, I dealt with intense loneliness. I used my willpower to hide the pain of my loneliness and sadness from myself, like I was being hidden in this hospital from the rest of the world.

The mental hospital seemed a lot like the images of jail that I saw on TV. Like a prison, I couldn't just leave, was stripped of my personal belongings, closely monitored by staff, and there were disciplinary consequences to acting out.

At the beginning of each new day in the hospital, I thought about the bribe my mother offered me. This motivated me to ask my parents to bring me a meal Taco Bell every time they visited, which was frequent, but not enough to feel like I wasn't all alone.

When I was bored at home, there was always something I could do about it, like play with Legos, go outside, or watch television. Being bored at the mental hospital was something completely different for me. There were less distractions to consume my time.

Several patients found ways to become distractions themselves by making jokes, acting out, or doing just about anything to not feel alone, lonely, and bored. Occasionally, a patient would go into a rage and "flip out" as we would say.

When this happened, the entire unit would go on lockdown, meaning all of the common areas were off limits and we would need to stay in our rooms or wherever we were when the lockdown happened. We would watch from afar as strong men restrained a screaming kid trying to claw their way out of their grasp like they were being hunted by a serial killer.

The fear of being punished and restrained helped keep me from even considering acting out while in the mental hospital. One of those consequences was "THE BED." According to rumors, "THE BED" was where hospital staff took patients when they were out of control.

No matter whom I talked to, from staff members to patients, there were different descriptions and stories about "THE BED" like an urban legend. I imagined it as a torture device where patients were chained and hung upside down until they begged to be let go or promised that they would behave.

I was first told about "THE BED" from another patient, who said it was behind the door across the hall from my room. After hearing about it, I would look to see if people went in or out of that room, but that rarely happened.

One day while walking by the room, I tried to open the door, but it was locked. There was a small window at the top of the door, but I could only see the ceiling since I was too short to get a better look at it.

Several days later, I left the day area where we are allowed to hang out to go back to my room for the evening. As I opened the door to my room, I froze with shock.

"THE BED" was not only a real thing, it was in my room and next to my bed! As I went to examine it up close, it looked like a really old hospital bed with the rails raised on all sides, like a prison cell and torture device combined. It had the same hideous dark green paint that was on the hospital walls, with rusty edges and a completely rusted out bottom. On the side of the bed were large metal cranks.

I wondered how many people had been restrained in this bed and what happens when someone is restrained. The next day, I nervously asked a staff member what the cranks were for. "They use the cranks to tighten the straps around your arms and legs when you get restrained," he said.

I never saw "THE BED" in action, thankfully, but we all knew when it was being used. I still have vivid memories of a hospital employee walking into the room with straps to hook onto the bed.

None of us could see it, but we all connected with what was going on and felt pain and empathy for the person being restrained. No one wants to see someone in that amount of pain.

There were many times when I was on the verge of going into a rage and flipping out, but the terrifying thought of "THE BED" motivated me to calm down. The other hospital efforts —medication, regular visits with a psychiatrist, a social worker, group therapy, and a classroom setting for school, probably helped as well, but nothing helped me behave myself more than the fear of "THE BED."

Even though I was never restrained in "THE BED", being in this cold, dark, lonely place was difficult. It was hard to believe that I belonged here—that anyone belongs in a place like this.

Did my parents and professionals really think this was the best way to help me get well? Did I really need to be isolated from the rest of society and remain a panic attack away from being strapped down with cranks and wrist straps on an old rusty bed?

I wanted my freedom back. I needed to get out of here the same way I had gotten here—by taking control of the situation.

Since I knew that breaking out wasn't an option, I started asking every adult that I encountered about going home. My persistence eventually paid off. I didn't get to go home just from asking, but they explained what I needed to work on in order to get out. I needed to better control my behavioral outbursts.

After several weeks of working hard to behave, I was discharged. I couldn't have been happier. I had been rehabilitated and had my freedom back.

When I reflect on my memories of 5th and 6th grade, I want to think about the excitement of the Teenage Mutant Ninja Turtles cartoon and movie. Those were the good memories but those years are also clouded by bad memories.

TRIGGER WARNING: This chapter contains a graphic description of a suicide attempt. Although I wanted to die at the time, I am so grateful that I lived.

CHAPTER 3

SPECIAL EDUCATION

Fresh air, freedom, unlimited TV time, and as much Taco Bell as I could eat—life on the outside of the mental hospital had never felt better. With just a over a month of summer time remaining, I made the most of it I before going back to school, taking nothing for granted. I was free!

Towards the end of the summer, my parents enrolled me in the local Boy Scouts of America, Troop 48. It just seemed like another activity my parents wanted me to do, but little did I know it would be good for me. Learning life skills, making friends, and spending time outdoors were all good for my development and mental health.

Boy Scout meetings were much more fun than attending Lutheran church, which we went to fairly regularly off and on for years.

Although I was kicked out of Sunday school for swearing, I enjoyed reading the Bible and learning about it. The lessons I learned through regularly attending church made me want to be a better person.

As much as I wanted to become the good, healthy person I knew I could be, new challenges started to appear. People in our neighborhood and some kids from my school knew where I had been for the past three weeks, and the thought of someone having to be in a mental hospital didn't come with many warm and fuzzy feelings.

The news of my stay getting out wasn't my parent's fault, as they tried their best to keep it secret. However, it's never easy to explain why your child has magically disappeared for a few weeks in the middle of summer.

As the news got out, parents of my friends wondered what I could've done, what I would grow up to be, and what kind of negative impact I would have on their children. They kept their children away from me like I had a contagious disease.

My parents, on the other hand, weren't treating me like I had a disease. They were willing to do whatever it took to get me to a better mental place and to see me succeed. When it came to school in the past, they had transferred me from one school to another, and nothing seemed to work except for one situation—receiving tutoring at home.

Working one-on-one with a private tutor wasn't a viable long-term solution because of the cost and the fact that it would isolate me from everyone else my age. However, it taught my parents that I needed individual attention, and not just because I craved it, but because when I worked with a teacher individually, I seemed to be at my best.

To get this type of attention for me in a supportive environment, my parents enrolled me in the Smith Street School's special education program. That's right, I was now in special education.

My fifth-grade year began in September of 1989 with me standing on the curb for the first day of school. A short yellow bus with tinted windows screeched to a stop near the curb. "Is this really where I belong?" I thought.

The idea of being in a special education class damaged my confidence, and it also came with a hurtful label. Not only was I "crazy" according to others , but now I was also "retarded," which was still an acceptable word at the time.

I began battling depression, struggling to maintain friendships, beginning puberty a little too soon, on medication (Tegretol, often used to treat Bipolar Disorder), changing schools once again, and now in special education. UGH!

Seeing the kids who were in the mainstream "normal class" every single day, I felt a surge of jealousy because they just seemed to have a "normal," fun school experience, while I felt like I was in a prison.

At the same time, I also felt judged because I was in special education. It seemed like all the boys in the other classes were cool and "normal." They knew how to dress, they were tough, and they played sports, and I wanted some of that. I was jealous of that.

Despite my emotional dysregulation, not everything was out of control. Although I was still acting out in school, my teacher knew exactly how to deal with me and handled these situations quickly. Needless to say, I still made a lot of trips to the principal's office, which were followed by suspensions and lectures from my father as he picked me up early from school.

In addition to "acting out," which came in the form of talking back and speaking when I wasn't supposed to, I discovered how much I enjoyed tapping my pencil on a desk. I could carry a rhythm, and the more I did it, the more I wanted to play the drums.

After annoying my teachers again and again with my pencil tapping, I was given an opportunity. If I behaved, which to the teacher meant earning gold stars, I could play drums! This was enough motivation for me to behave, and I was allowed to begin learning how to play the drums in the fifth grade.

When I was in band class, I was at peace. Being able to actually play drums allowed me to concentrate my negative energy on something positive. I started to gain the trust of my teacher and my parents.

My parents even let me stay home after school when they weren't there. I would go into my mother's room when I got home, lay out on her big comfortable bed, and watch cartoons like *DuckTales*, *Teenage Mutant Ninja Turtles* (TMNT), and *Animaniacs*.

This was a great way to spend the afternoon before my mom came home from work. But when she got home, it was hard to know what to predict. Some days were good, some days were bad, and I never knew which mother I would get, so when it got closer to when she would get home, I would feel my heart begin to race. On her toughest days, I could feel a dark and negative energy in her that would spill over from her to me, changing my mood as well.

At school, drumming gave me a positive outlet for my emotions, but at home things were different. At home, I unleashed my rage by yelling, throwing tantrums or breaking things. None of that made the pain I felt go away. Worst of all, I couldn't understand why I felt so much hurt and pain inside.

It felt like an increasing amount of weight and pressure, but it wasn't on top of my shoulders. It felt more like a heavy, negative energy stuck in my stomach and chest that held me down.

The frustration I felt from this negative energy day after day caused me to seek out more outlets outside of drumming. I wanted this feeling to go away and was willing to do whatever it took to get rid of it, but didn't know how.

My parents, counselors, and psychiatrists worked to take my pain away through counseling sessions and medication. And if medication could be used in small doses to help ease my mind, then why couldn't a large amount of medication make me feel much better quicker? Maybe it would be better to be dead.

On Friday, September 29, 1989, I went looking for that quick solution. After coming home from school with no one else in the house, I walked over to the medicine cabinet where I knew my mom kept my pills.

Each day, I would take one pill in the morning with breakfast. But the intense and overwhelming pain I felt wasn't going to go away with a single pill. I needed a more drastic and immediate solution.

I grabbed the pill bottle, worked to get it open, and swallowed the 25 pills left in the bottle. I didn't necessarily want to die; I wanted a solution to the pain, and this seemed like the solution.

After taking the pills, I continued my normal after school routine, and went into my mother's room to watch cartoons on her bed. About an hour later, I felt a warm and calm feeling come over me. It made me incredibly tired, and I dozed off into a nap.

"Oh my God! You're going to die," my mother said as she grabbed and shook me. She had found the empty bottle near the medicine cabinet and me asleep in her bed.

She didn't waste a second in picking me up and rushing out of the house to the hospital. She may not have been there for me much emotionally, but she was there to drive me to the hospital in time to save my life.

At the hospital, we rushed into an emergency room. I felt calm and relaxed, but everyone around me was running around frantically and noticeably concerned. That calm feeling didn't last long as a plastic tube was shoved through my nose down into my stomach.

This was the most uncomfortable, painful, and out of control feeling I have ever had in my life. After a coal solution was pumped down the tube, I vomited up everything in my system again and again.

The nurses and doctor were pleased with how I was reacting after having my stomach pumped, so I was moved from the emergency room to intensive care. Shortly after being transferred to intensive care, a well-dressed woman with a concerned look on her face approached me.

"Hello, Michael. I see that you were in the psychiatric unit of the hospital a few months ago. We will need to reevaluate you because you may need to go back," she said. Images of "THE BED," being watched at all times, and being stripped of my freedom flashed through my head.

There was no way I could let them take me back. I knew that at that moment I had to more persuasive than I had ever been in my life.

"No, it was just a big mistake," I said. "I promise you: this will NEVER happen again!" A few questions later, I had somehow convinced the psychiatrist that I was fit to return home instead of making another trip to the mental hospital.

This was one of my greatest accomplishments at that time. I

gained a false sense of control from being able to convince her that I was OK, but I knew deep down inside that I still needed help as I was still in so much pain. The calm from the pills had worn off, and my solution to get rid of the pain had failed.

Similar to my hospitalization several months earlier, my parents kept this incident a family secret. Even close extended family members, like Uncle Billy, didn't know. I appreciated that they didn't want the rest of the world to know what I was going through, but at the same time, I wished people in my life cared about me enough to know.

After my suicide attempt, I began going to weekly therapy sessions with my parents. These were not fun experiences, but it was time I got to spend with my parents outside of the house, and it started to work, at least to some extent. I began to feel better, control my anger, and find some joy in life—mainly through girls.

I had a crush on a girl named Jessica. I was in love with her and she ignored my existence. I would stare at her, try to start conversations, and send her love notes in class.

She never responded, which made me want her even more. Looking back on this crush, the scariest part of this situation, more than my constant unwelcomed love notes that I sent her, is that Jessica looked exactly like my mother.

During the summer between fifth and sixth grade, my parents enrolled me in a day camp in a town nearby. This was my first experience being in a day camp with other kids that were "normal", and I had a blast.

Before registering me for camp, my mother met with the camp administrators and probably told them about some of my challenges. Ironically, the camp actually offered me a job to do before camp.

I would arrive to camp early, do some cleaning, and make some money for the summer. I saved all of the earnings from my camp job. That summer came and left in an instant. In the blink of an eye, my sixth grade school year was beginning.

My infatuation with Jessica the year before, surprisingly, was not the most awkward interaction I would have with a young woman at this point in my life. There was also a girl on the bus I flirted with on the ride home. On one regretful ride home, I worked up enough courage to flash her, which at the time I must have thought was somehow a romantic gesture instead of indecent exposure.

As you can imagine, and rightfully so, she was horrified and told her parents and the school. It became clear that I was not very good at interacting with women or knowing how to act properly towards them. After my suspension for indecent exposure, I decided to concentrate on other things, and once again, life started looking a little bit brighter.

But I still found myself in the principal's office when I had occasional behavioral outbursts like swearing at my teacher and occasionally throwing a desk. This would be followed by my dad having to come pick me up from school because suspension was the consequence for my behavior.

My dad would drive all the way from work, pick me up, and take me back to work. I knew this was probably not good for him or his job security, but I knew that I couldn't control my behavior. Although I was better than I was in fourth grade, I still struggled to behave.

During this school year, the *Teenage Mutant Ninja Turtle* movie came out and I couldn't have been more excited. I would often watch the *Teenage Mutant Ninja Turtle* cartoon after school.

Each turtle had a different personality: Leonardo was the leader,

Donatello was the nerd, Raphael was emotional, and Michaelangelo was a goofball. I identified with Raphael and Michaelangelo.

The movie was amazing. I wanted to be a superhero just like them and thought that drumming was my path to becoming a superhero.

My drumming began to improve, and the school band had an opening. I felt like the crazy, retarded kid outside of the band room, but in it, I was an equal with the other students. They saw my talent and passion for drumming, and it helped me build confidence and start friendships with several kids in the class.

In addition to my band teacher, my general music teacher also recognized my growth and interest in drumming. She looked out for me in class and talked to me about music, my life outside of band, and faith.

One day, she sent me home with Jehovah's Witness pamphlets, which my mother did not appreciate. When it came time to graduate from the sixth grade, she invited me to accompany her as she played piano and performed at graduation, which was an honor and something I was very proud of.

Graduation meant that I would need to find another school. As a reward for my improvement and good behavior, my parents decided that it was time for me to try a private school again and leave the "special education" aspect of my life behind me.

This time, they didn't just decide amongst themselves and tell me where I was going to go to school. Instead, they let me pick what school I wanted to go to. I went from feeling like an insecure kid to more of a teenager with options and responsibilities.

I made the decision of what school to go to based on my Christian faith. No, I wasn't called by God to pick a specific school; I wanted to grow in my faith and give religion a more serious chance to have a positive impact on my life.

In the past, we went as a family to church about once a week. Although I didn't feel like I got much out of it, I was willing to give faith another chance, and I chose a private Lutheran school, Long Island Lutheran Jr./Sr. High School, also known as LuHi. Fortunately, there were no school uniforms, but there was a dress code.

When we visited the school, the overall feel of the school was positive and relaxed rather than restrictive, like the Catholic school from my past. I saw this as another opportunity for a clean start. I was out of special education, far removed from my hospitalization and suicide attempt, and ready to move forward.

During the summer between sixth and seventh grade, I began taking private drum lessons in my band teacher's home. My mom joined me as I got to learn how to play my first beat on the drums.

It was so difficult to coordinate all three limbs. Luckily, I didn't have to use all four yet. The beat I learned was called the basic rock beat, which is the simplest and most popular drum beat in American music.

Since I didn't have drums at home, I sat outside at the picnic table and tapped it out. For weeks, I would try to master this pattern. It was frustrating, but I truly believed that I could master it. I understood it in my head but my limbs were just not lining up.

I was excited for the next stage in my life.

A fresh start in a new school was just what I needed. In the following chapter, you'll learn how I responded to that transition.

My emotional pain and suffering got worse.

TRIGGER WARNING: This chapter contains a description of self-harm.

CHAPTER 4

SOUTH OAKS HOSPITAL

"But we're never gonna survive unless we get a little crazy." On the first day of the seventh grade, I heard Seal's hit song "Crazy" on the radio, and it connected with me in a special way. Maybe a little bit of crazy was okay, and maybe I was going to be okay.

I had high expectations. I felt older, wiser, and was excited to be in a new school once again. Forget about just trying to fit in—I believed I was going to make the football team, play in the band, and get a hot girlfriend all in my first year.

Even with my sky-high hopes, the year started better than I could've hoped for. I met new friends, chased the elusive "hot girlfriend," and was doing well in the classroom. I paid attention in each class, was respectful of my teachers, and started to really enjoy school, which I didn't believe was even possible before.

After school, I would take the bus home, and as I walked in the front door of my house, my happiness dimmed as if someone had turned down the volume of joy I had felt at school.

On the inside, although I tried to hide it with fake smiles and "I'm good" responses to "how are you?" I felt sad and worthless—like someone who had been convinced they weren't going to amount to anything and had nobody to love them. That wasn't true. I had people who loved and looked out for me but that did little to change the growing pain that was once again building up inside me.

The pain started to turn into dangerous behaviors. At night, I would steal my dad's shaving razors. I'd take them to my room, close the door, and begin to self-harm, hoping the feeling that haunted me would escape along with the blood in my arms.

The external pain somehow temporarily eased my internal pain for a few seconds but then I would eventually return to feeling depressed. The pain grew steadily, and not even the self-harm could make a difference in this internal agony.

When I began self-harming, I was dating a girl in my class named Rachel. One day after school, Rachel and I were together in the hall with no one else around. I spontaneously decided to take out razor I had brought to school and self-harm in front of her.

I remember her getting really upset, and I know it was very traumatizing for her to experience that. To this day, it's something that I deeply regret.

At home, I would scream at the top of my lungs and break things in my bedroom. The pain kept growing. I didn't only want to hurt myself; I wanted to hurt anyone and anything that came into my path.

Bruce Banner was no longer in sight and a Hulk-like being had taken full control. He wanted to hurt me, my parents, and my younger brother, and he began to crave destruction. One violent instance led to another, and they soon became a regular occurrence.

Each outburst became increasingly more violent. I was smart enough to see the dangerous path I was on, but not emotionally intelligent enough to do anything about it except to continue letting the pain out.

The movie version of this aspect of my life was approaching its grand finale. My dad, whom I often viewed as the tough no-nonsense villain, was frustrated and reaching his breaking point. One night, I attacked him with everything I had. I yelled, threw things, swore at him left and right with no intention of backing off.

In order to see how far I could get with my dad, I walked right up to him and yelled at him. I quickly found myself on the floor with him on top of me.

Slap!

My dad's right hand connected with my face. I couldn't let him know it had an impact on me. "Go f*** yourself," I said.

Spit!

My spit landed right in his face, and I followed it up with a challenge. "Do it again," I said.

Bam!

Another slap from the villain, my father. I was resisting with all of my power, but he wasn't willing to lose this battle, just as I wouldn't admit defeat.

"Ahahahahahahahaha!" My best countermove was to laugh in his face. I felt I couldn't lose if I didn't let him know I was hurt.

By now, it was clear that I was the villain and not my father. And what do you do with a classic comic book-like villain? You put them behind bars.

He picked me up, forced me into his car, and drove to South Oaks Hospital, a residential psychiatric hospital on Long Island.

Because of my violent behavior and self-harm, I was admitted to South Oaks Hospital and placed on suicide watch. My first three days were spent in a bedroom with a see-through glass wall, no shoelaces, and without anything that could possibly be used to hurt myself. I was under constant surveillance and stripped of all privacy.

I felt pathetic. I didn't know why other patients were in the hospital, but I was one of only two people on suicide watch out of more than twenty people in the unit. I mean, come on, I wasn't really going to kill myself.

I may have told my parents that I was going to, but that doesn't mean I would go through with it, or would I? By being In South Oaks, I was already separated from the rest of society. Now I was further singled out as a freak—a freak among freaks.

For the second time in my life, I had to adjust to life in a mental hospital. In all fairness to the staff at South Oaks Hospital tried their best to make the environment "normal."

Like school, announcements over a loudspeaker were part of our daily routine. Some announcements were normal updates and others were due to an emergency. The number sequence 2 2 2 was used over the sound system to indicate an emergency in one of the units.

If the code was "2 2 2 Code Blue," there was a medical emergency. If it was "2 2 2 Code Red," there was a fire.

The third emergency code they used was "2 2 2 Code Green," which meant that one of the patients was out of control and needed to be restrained by staff. Being restrained came with straps and an injection of Thorazine into their veins.

The first time I heard "2 2 2 Code Green on Northwest 2" was a surreal experience. It was as if my nightmares about "THE BED" from the other mental hospital were playing out in real life.

The big metal doors to the unit burst open, and several huge guys in white uniforms came running down the hall. They approached the room like a SWAT team taking down a dangerous criminal. As they opened the door, one ran in and grabbed the patient while the other looked for a way to help get them on the bed.

They then proceeded to restrain the patient while the nurse came in and reached for her needle. All of the other patients were escorted out of the area. In my mind, they were just getting rid of witnesses.

A few seconds later the patient's screams turned into silence. This scenario, which happened many times during my stay, was difficult to watch.

It was like a scene in a horror movie where you cover your eyes so you can blur the line from reality to fiction. Unfortunately, this was all too real.

As much as I acted out at home, I never got out of control while in the hospital. I knew what would happen if I did, and I didn't want any part of "2 2 2 Code Green." My attitude at the hospital was far different from what I displayed at home.

By keeping my cool and doing my best to control my emotions, I was eventually taken off suicide watch. I immediately felt better being able to sleep with a little privacy and relax. This took me from a place or worry and fear, because I was being monitored 24/7, to a place of calm, where I could, at the very least, think without having someone watch me think through a glass wall.

Days went by, and new experiences turned into routines. Part of our weekly routine included a trip to the fitness center.

Having access to a fitness center and a trainer at a mental hospital was never something I would've imagined. Here I was "hospitalized," and I had access to a gym. And this was a real gym, complete with Nautilus machines and brand new equipment.

I asked my parents to send me bodybuilding magazines and drum magazines. Those were the two things I got excited about: drumming and bodybuilding. After seeing my first bodybuilding magazine, I realized that I want a body like that.

At the time, I didn't realize many of the people in those magazines used drugs to become extremely muscular and ripped. Regardless, it gave me something to aspire to that made me feel good. I wanted the body of a superhero.

Inspired, I began to work out at least three times a week. Over time, I noticed changes in my muscle mass, which gave me a boost in self-esteem, energy, and confidence.

It was addicting, and I pushed myself harder and harder. I started to feel better about myself, and I could tell others recognized this change, including the girls on my unit.

My unit was called Northwest 2, a coed unit for teenagers. The unit had community rules to ensure safety and to control the atmosphere. Every patient started with Level 1 privileges.

If you followed the rules and earned the trust of the staff, you moved to Level 2. When you moved to Level 2, you were "rewarded" with a later curfew, access to a separate unsupervised day area, and the ability to go outside. These all seem like minor comforts, but when in a mental hospital, the difference between Level 1 and Level 2 was like choosing between a rotten cabbage and a steak for dinner.

I got my first crack at romance the day Samantha was admitted to Northwest 2. Usually, when a new patient entered the unit, they went through a period of shame and shyness. By looking at their face, I could tell how much pain they were in. Some were noticeably more depressed than I ever was, and I felt bad for them. I knew what it felt like to be in pain, and pain is what caused all of us to get sent here.

However, when Samantha entered the unit, she walked proudly without any shame or shyness. This got my attention. Samantha had everything I was looking for at that time: she was a girl, had nice legs, was accessible, and seemed to show a mutual interest in me.

A few weeks after she arrived, we began "dating," which is a far different experience from a relationship outside of a mental hospital. Still, it still made me feel confident and special. Dating as a patient doesn't really make a relationship all that different than relationships with other patients, but she and I secretly knew the difference.

Samantha eventually got Level 2 privileges. She and I took advantage of any opportunity to show affection under our Level 2 privileges. We were curious, and got away with quite a lot when staff members had their backs turned, from quick kisses to full make out and groping sessions.

I knew Samantha wasn't the love of my life, but I enjoyed our time together. We were a couple of young rebels exploring forbidden love. Well, not love, but you get the picture.

A couple of months into our relationship, the party ended. We were "discovered" by a staff member "acting inappropriately." The rules didn't have much wiggle room for physical relationships, and the staff forced us to separate.

After the staff-forced breakup, we were both monitored heavily. She soon stopped showing me the same affection and attention, and it hit me hard. Even though we were often in the same room together, emotionally, we were miles apart.

I started to miss the attention, affection, stimulation, and the pleasure I got from our interactions, and it hurt. I went from being on top of the world to feeling like a piece of dirt. My experience with her set a precedent for future relationships with women, and it also helped me understand the emotional highs and lows I would experience on a regular basis going in and out of relationships.

There were many high and lows during my stay at South Oaks Hospital. As I progressed in my treatment, I started to get additional privileges. On Christmas Day, I got a pass to spend an entire day with my family; it was a great day.

My parents got me the best Christmas gift ever—a new drum set! Going back to the hospital toward the end of Christmas day and leaving my family and drums behind was especially difficult. I knew that, overall, things were getting better, but there was no guarantee I would get discharged anytime soon.

Eventually, I was granted weekend passes. My dad would pick me up Friday right before dinner, and I could stay home until Sunday. On those weekends, I spent most of my time in my parents' basement playing drums.

I would work on new drum beats and play along to music on the radio for the entire time. This made me feel so good, and I started to feel like I was building up momentum towards getting better.

While growing as a drummer helped, my real break came when I received my official diagnosis—Narcissistic Personality Disorder. I had known for quite a while that I was different; however, this was the first time someone explained it to me, and this served as the beginning of understanding myself.

While I've been told that it's not appropriate to give this diagnosis to a patient before the age of eighteen, and many professionals have disagreed with my diagnosis, it was helpful to me at the time. Mental health challenges are confusing.

I met many counselors and therapists during my time in psychiatric hospitals, but none as memorable as Dr. T from South Oaks. Dr. T was in his mid-50's, had a thick beard, and grey hair. He looked like a stereotypical psychiatrist from a movie, but the way he cared for me and others was far from typical based on my many experiences.

Dr. T listened to what I said carefully, and I truly felt that he understood me. He didn't just ask questions to write prescriptions; he was genuinely interested, patient, kind, and funny. The other counselors and psychiatrists I had in the past weren't necessarily bad, Dr. T just had a special way of connecting on a deeper level with me.

To Dr. T, I wasn't just another troubled youth; I was a human being. Seeing him each week while I was there gave me a profound sense of comfort.

In addition to Dr. T, I began to develop rapport with one of the staff members. His name was Joe, and he was a drummer too. Our conversations about drumming were one of the best parts of my stay at South Oaks Hospital. After many conversations, he gave me a pair of Pro-Mark 747 Neil Peart drumsticks, which is still one of my favorite drumsticks to use.

Eventually, I was fully discharged from South Oaks after six very long months.

My stay at South Oaks taught me a lot. I received a reminder that acting out leads to long hospital stays with no freedom, a fitness lifestyle that became an important component for both my recovery and my life, attention from a woman, a diagnosis, and a doctor that understood me and gave me hope.

In addition to what I was able to learn and experience, my family received benefits as well. They got a better-behaved child. My diagnosis also gave them answers and an explanation as to why I acted out and had a need for control.

In this chapter, I ride a roller coaster of behavior and emotions all the way through high school. Somewhere along this ride, I discovered what really makes me happy and my life began to take a different direction.

Getting discharged from South Oaks Hospital began a new season in my life—a season of self discovery.

CHAPTER 5

DRUMMING

I was on my best behavior as I finished out seventh grade. I had a new sense of freedom and wasn't going to give it back anytime soon. I was respectful to teachers, nice to my parents, and tried my hardest in class. But I was still a twelve-year-old boy who was growing in odd ways, and I didn't have the maturity to act like a responsible adult.

Regrettably, as I walked past a classmate after school, I said, "Man, she's got some big ass tits." My comment hadn't fallen on deaf ears. "Excuse me?" she said. The young woman, Julie, heard exactly what I said, and she wasn't amused. My heart sank deep down into my stomach, and I felt terrible.

At the time, I was more upset that I got caught than the fact that

I said it, but her reaction and the way I felt made me question why I said it. "I'm really sorry" was all I could think to say. She still wasn't happy, but seemed to accept my apology.

The rest of the seventh grade went much smoother than my ability to speak to women. I kept myself disciplined and out of trouble and had plenty to look forward to going into the summer.

That summer was full of day camp, counseling sessions, and lots of basketball and baseball. I wasn't very good at sports, but getting away from the house was always good. My parents figured that I wouldn't have time to act out if they kept me busy, and they were right.

I was getting fresh air and exercise, and I was learning a lot, both through counseling sessions with Dr. T, who I continued to work with, and camp where I began to develop better social skills.

That summer flew by and 8th grade came with more change. On the better side of things, I got a girlfriend. Believe it or not, my distasteful comment to Julie in the 7th grade, followed by an apology, eventually led to her being my first real girlfriend, and she was gorgeous.

She was also very passionate about social causes, including affirmative action and gender equality. Having someone involved in causes like this in my life helped me understand their importance and become more well-rounded.

The excitement and self-esteem boost that came with having the "hot girlfriend" rubbed off on other areas of my life. My drumming skills and reputation both started to grow. People knew me as "Mike, the Drummer," and I started getting more attention from the music teacher who encouraged me to work hard and improve my skills.

Not all changes during this time were positive. A few months into the school year, my father was laid off from his job as a customs broker for an international shipping company. In our household, my father brought in over twice as much money as my mother, who was an executive assistant at Hofstra University at the time.

The layoff had nothing to do with his performance, and he tried very hard to limit its impact on the family. However, my mother took every opportunity to make sure he felt ashamed for it like it was his fault. He took it all in stride without ever fighting back or even responding to her.

Since I thought my mother was always right, I also started to blame him, feeling like he was a loser. How my mother treated my dad made me want to be anything but him. In my interactions with women, I worked hard to avoid women looking down on me or putting me down.

This desire to not be like him lead to me aggressively taking control of tense situations, like when I got in trouble in class. I needed to show that I was in charge of the situation and would not be talked down to or made out to be a loser. This is one reason I'm a workaholic today: I never want someone to look at me the way my mom looked at my dad.

After his layoff, he worked several small jobs before eventually landing something close to his previous position and pay level. Despite the job stress at home, I finished my 8th grade year with good grades and very few behavior problems.

My father wasn't the only male I had to look up (or down) to. During the following school year, in 9th grade, despite being on a much tighter budget, my parents hired one of the best drum teachers on Long Island to tutor me. They told him about my struggle staying in school, mental health challenges, and stays in psychiatric hospitals.

He knew exactly how to get the most out of me, pushing and challenging me in every way. Each session was videotaped. Skip, the teacher, would make me watch and analyze our lessons on video to see what I was doing right and where I could improve.

On his wall, Skip had a poster with the words "Be Each Note" on it. He taught me that every moment was important both when playing the drums and in life. Any small lapse or taking a moment for granted wasn't good enough for Skip.

He was the alternative figure to my dad, who I struggled with in two ways—I saw him as the villain in my struggles, and my mom always made him out to be a problem.

After reaching the peak of having the hot girlfriend, being recognized for my skills as a drummer, and working with one of the best drum teachers in Long Island, my life started trending downwards once again. My girlfriend, Julie, left for a different school at the start of 9th grade, so we broke up.

Our relationship during the school year before had given me a lot of confidence, which started to wear off. I missed feeling the special attention she gave me. The letdown from the end of this relationship didn't cause me to immediately fall off of an emotional cliff, but I was starting to slip.

Home continued to bring out the worst in me. The daily guessing game of which mother I would get when she came home made it difficult to even want to be there.

There was no social stability, and it was unpredictable, unlike what school had now become for me. Away from the structure that school provided, I didn't know what to do with my feelings once again.

Nothing in life made me feel good except for music. Music offered me a way to fit in, and it was no different when I got into the 10th grade. During that year, I was the drummer in my school's jazz band.

We had been preparing for weeks for a special competition in Boston. Our band made the trip from New York to the competition, which was held at the Berklee School of Music.

My parents took the four-hour trip north to watch us perform a brief twenty-minute routine. It was a short performance, but they wanted to show their support, and it meant the world to me.

Leading up to the performance, I had worked for months to memorize each piece note for note, feeling focused and ready to give the drum performance of a lifetime. I was the only drummer in the band and, thus, had full creative freedom.

My four limbs had to move quickly in relaxed coordination to get the right sound out of each drum and cymbal with the right timing and touch. During the first song, after getting off to what I thought was a great start, I could tell something was off with the drum set I was playing.

As I looked up during the middle of the song, one of the cymbals had come loose and was coming towards my head. In the nick of time, I caught it right before it could make a loud crash and ruin our chance of impressing the judges with our performance. Fortunately, I managed to keep the song going smoothly.

Shortly after our performance, I learned that our band did not impress the judges, and we left the competition without any accolades. However, in reading over their notes, they commented that the drummer "drove the band well." I did that—that was me!

I was sad that our band didn't win anything, but receiving that validation from the critical judges confirmed that my hard work had paid off, and that I was at least good for something.

This feeling soon faded. After coming off of the high of the competition, I had nothing to look forward to. I had to face the immediate reality of my surroundings and the current loneliness in my life.

I began having a tough time in school; I didn't want to do my work, my love life was non-existent, I was angry, and I couldn't connect with the other kids in school. I was occasionally bullied by the popular kids, and I began acting out towards my teachers.

The school year was full of loneliness and hurt that caused me to act out both verbally and physically. As bad as school was, being at home was still worse, especially at night. I was in such emotional pain that I could feel it in my chest. As I tried to fall asleep, I would lie awake still feeling empty, upset, and wondering why I couldn't be happy.

During the night, I would frequently sneak out of my parent's house and go on mini late-night rampages to let out my frustration. I hurled rocks at cars, broke windows, threw sticks, whatever I could do to temporarily forget about my emptiness.

In those moments of vandalism, I lost all fear and truly didn't care if I got caught. At some level, I wanted to get caught by the police or a neighbor, just to be noticed for the damage I was causing.

On one of those nights, I was overwhelmed with anger and determined to do something. A few blocks away from my house, I saw a local elementary school. I walked up to the front of the school and checked the doors—they were locked.

I walked around to the side and then to the back of the school where I faced two solid metal doors with old, outdated locks.

I reached in my back pocket and grabbed my school ID card. Sliding the card in n front of the lock, I was able to open the door.

I walked into a room that looked like a large industrial supplies closet. There were stacks of old rusty paint cans, tool boxes, empty cardboard boxes, and spare parts on shelves. As I looked around, I saw a bright red box that read "Fire Alarm, Pull Down."

It was practically calling my name. Pulling the alarm was my chance to get the attention I needed and to show everyone what level of damage I could do. I took both hands, and with a smile, pulled down the alarm.

I knew exactly what I was doing, but still, the deafening sound made me jump. As the alarm echoed throughout the school hallways, I felt a sense of pride. This was my baby—something I did.

I caused this to happen, and I was damn proud of it. I slowly walked to the door, pushed it open as hard as I could, then proceeded to head back toward the street, and sat down on the curb facing the school.

Nothing was going to please me as much as seeing the look on the police officers' faces as they arrested me for what I had done. I sat and waited.

I was ready to spend my night in jail. I looked forward to my parents' anger and disappointment, the attention it would bring, almost as much as showing the police that *I was in control*.

Two minutes after I first pulled the alarm, I could hear sirens. Soon, I could see lights. Two fire trucks and a police car were coming down the street.

This was my moment. The police car, ahead of the fire trucks, swerved around the block, and parked about fifty feet in front of me right in front of the school.

The police and firefighters didn't notice me sitting on the curb when they pulled up. They stepped out of their vehicles to inspect the school. Going into the building, the firemen took their time looking around to make sure that no one was there.

When they cleared the school, making sure no one was inside, they shut the alarm off and walked out, coming right towards me. I stared right at them without looking away. They needed to know that even though they *could* arrest me, it was *my choice* to be caught.

I was in control. I sat up tall and didn't break my focus or turn my head. The officer, who was the first one out of the school, came within a few feet of me and looked right in my eyes... and then turned his back. He walked to his car and got inside.

Next came the firemen. To make sure they didn't look past me, I stood up. But still, like the policeman, they walked right past me and drove away.

What the hell? A young black teenager sitting right in front of a school that was broken into doesn't even get questioned? Did I need to run to get their attention?

Needless to say, this was the least satisfying act of defiance in my attention-seeking misdemeanor history. The last thing I wanted was to get away with it.

I rushed back to my house and called 911. "I set off the alarm," I said as I hung up the phone.

Five minutes later, the police were at my front door, and this time, they weren't looking past me. "Did you call 911!?" my dad asked. "No," I replied with a big smile across my face. Everyone knew that I was lying, but that's what I wanted.

As silly as it seems now, I still feel victorious about this event. In a world where I often felt and still feel out of control, this made me feel in charge. I don't even regret the stress I caused my parents, the wasted public resources, or distracting the fire department from a real emergency.

I won something that night. I was able to separate myself from the terrible feeling of emptiness I battled every day, even if just for a few hours.

I continued to act out more and more during the second half of the school year. My parents tried everything, and they still didn't know how to handle me. The more they "helped," the more I wanted them to feel the wrath of my pain.

They took away privileges, yelled, threatened, and bribed me with Taco Bell, which failed yet again. My reward came in frustrating them and taking control of situations. They couldn't give me a reward—it was something I had to take.

Nearly every week there was a new psychiatric emergency. Each time, my dad and I would end up in the same place—in the car on the way to the emergency room at Nassau County Medical Center. Out of the ten or so trips I made to the ER that year, every experience was exactly the same.

We walked into the waiting area, checked-in, and waited. Several hours later, a nurse would take us back into a room and ask the same dumb questions.

After a few visits, I memorized every detail about the Nassau County Medical Center emergency room—from the uncomfortable seats to the vomit green walls. The staff and I were even on a first-name basis, but I doubt they were happy to see me so regularly.

Although I knew I intentionally acted out, part of me wondered why this kept happening. As I sat and waited to see the psychiatrist on duty, I visualized achieving my primary goal: avoid being hospitalized.

The majority of the time, I was successful. However, achieving this goal became impossible with the way I was challenging my parents and acting out. Once again, I was eventually admitted to the psychiatric unit of Nassau County Medical Center on April 27th, 1995.

This was an achievement and a punishment. I was trying to stay out of the hospital, but I deserved and earned every trip there. The worst part of being in the mental hospital this time was missing the big drum clinic my dad had planned to take me to. Drumming was the best part of life, and having it taken away was the one thing that hurt more than the emotional pain that I was going through.

I was admitted to the exact same unit I was admitted to in the summer after 4th grade. I could never feel comfortable in a hospital. However, I was starting to feel like I belonged.

The floor above me was the adult unit. If still hospitalized at the age of 18, I would move upstairs, which seemed much more like a jail than a place that helps you get mentally fit for life outside. I was terrified of the idea of being hospitalized for any period of time as an adult, and the thought of being there for the rest of my life was terrifying.

But if I *was* going to be here for a while, I might as well try to make friends. I've made several short-term friends that I'll never forget, like Marshall. Marshall was a patient in the unit with me. He was several years younger and had a developmental disability. He was angered easily and was always getting yelled at by the staff for one thing or another, but he usually behaved.

Being teenage boys, we took every opportunity to make fun of each other. One evening, a few of us were in the hallway, laughing at Marshall, and he became extremely agitated. His agitation turned into rage, and he threatened and then tried to attack us.

After a couple of minutes, the staff came down the hall to restrain him. Three men came and pushed him into his room, forced him down on the bed, and strapped him to the rails. A nurse was behind them with a needle.

We sat there and watched his eyes roll back in his head as the Thorazine went into his bloodstream. The bed was his own, but this image was just as terrifying as THE BED that was here the last time.

A few days later, Marshall said something that made me think about how I perceived myself and the other patients. We were talking about some of the other patients in our ward, and he referred to one of them as "crazy."

"Crazy?" I thought. If we're all locked up in the mental hospital, aren't we all crazy?

Whether I was crazy or just going through a rough period, I wasn't sure I had the potential to become anything other than a mental hospital patient. I expressed these feelings and my concerns about having no hope to the teacher who spent time giving us academic instruction every weekday.

She handed me a sheet of paper with a single quote on it, "You never fail until you stop trying," by Albert Einstein. I paused and thought about it for a while.

Maybe I wasn't a failure after all. Maybe I wasn't crazy; I just needed to keep trying.

If I kept trying, I could possibly overcome my behavior problems. I might have a chance to beat my depression. I could maybe even have real friends.

For the first time in my life, I felt a glimmer of hope… real hope, unlike the hope I had felt in the past.

I knew that I was ready to deal with my life and didn't want to spend the rest of my it in a mental hospital. The thought of going home and starting over was exciting.

After being in a mental hospital for weeks, I wasn't thinking about the things that made me sad and angry or my behavior, which lead to me getting hospitalized. I missed having freedom and playing drums.

Like most teenagers, I always felt like I didn't have enough freedom; that everyone was controlling me and not letting me be myself. It's funny how much you miss something once it's actually gone.

This made me realize how much freedom I had before being admitted to the hospital. I desperately wanted back what I once had and the chance to take my life in a new direction. Most importantly, for the first time, I was willing to put in the work.

I took every opportunity to ask the staff about getting discharged, hoping that my perseverance would pay off. I finally got an answer, but it wasn't the answer I was looking for. I was told to write a letter stating my desire, detailing why I felt that I should be discharged.

Writing this letter would come with a lot of risk. If my request was accepted, I would be free to leave. If rejected, I would be forced to stay in the hospital, or I could go to court and fight it, which was a scary thought.

With a pattern of behavior, along with my history of going in and out of emergency rooms and hospitals, I knew that going to court would not go well. Both the court and the hospital had every reason to keep me there, send me to a residential treatment facility, or a group home if my letter was rejected.

Writing this letter became my one focus. I worked hard on carefully crafting what I would write.

I needed another chance to prove that I could live in society and make a positive difference in the world, and this was it. For a week, I wrote draft after draft focusing on my wording, grammar, and making sure it came from the heart. I then sent the letter.

After what seemed to be forever, I receive a written response. The letter gave a date and time for me to meet face-to-face with a panel of doctors to determine if I would stay hospitalized for the foreseeable future or be released.

The day of the meeting finally arrived. I walked into a dimly lit room where a table full of doctors were sitting down wearing hospital gowns. "So, you want to be discharged?" one asked.

That question caught me off guard, and it seemed a little odd for two reasons. First, I wouldn't have written the letter or showed up for the meeting if I didn't want to be discharged. Secondly, who the hell would want to stay in a place like this?

"Yes," I said confidently after thinking about it for a few seconds. I was nervous, but I knew that I could show them I deserved to be released.

One of them said to me, "Michael, you are a smart guy. You know that your behavior is not good, yet you continue to choose to act out. You can stay in the hospital for the rest of your life or not. It's your choice."

He was right. I explained to them that my choice was to not spend the rest of my life in a mental hospital. I promised that I would make the changes needed so I would never have to come back, and I meant it.

They knew, at some level, that I was trying to give them the answers I thought they wanted to hear. But they also knew that I could be successful outside of the unit if I actually tried, which I was prepared to do.

On May 17, 1995, just a few days after meeting with the doctors, I was discharged from the mental hospital at Nassau County Medical Center. There was just a few weeks left in the school year, and I was excited for summer.

At the end of a very difficult year, a summer packed full of distractions and healthy outlets was exactly what I needed. On that first day of summer break, I watched cartoons in the morning while eating a gigantic bowl of cereal, went out to play basketball, and then watched some more cartoons. When my mom got home, she held up a manila envelope and said, "We got a letter from your school."

I had no clue what the letter could be about, but curiously asked her if I could open it. I opened the envelope and began to read the letter, which came from the school board. "Dear Mr. & Mrs. Veny, we regret to inform you that your child Michael is no longer welcome...."

I couldn't read the rest before tearing up, knowing that I had just been expelled from yet another school. The letter went on to explain that not only was I expelled, but the school board would not allow an appeal of their decision.

Suddenly, everything hit me at once in what became one of the most devastating days of my entire life. Everything positive was taken away from me. I now knew I was destined to be a failure.

I had been expelled from three schools, had just completed my third stay at a mental hospital, had a history of acting out violently, self-harming regularly, couldn't make real friends, and had attempted suicide.

At the end of 10th grade, I felt like my life might as well be over. I was supposedly going into the 11th grade, but I didn't have a school to go to.

My parents were also having a difficult time, and now they had to try to find a school that would accept me.

A couple of weeks later, I was getting some fresh air while bouncing a basketball in our driveway. My mom came out of the house with my dad close behind her.

"What do you want to do about school for next year?" she asked. I could tell that they both really wanted me to finish high school, without adding any suspensions or expulsions to my record.

I thought for a second about what I really wanted out of school. "How about I quit school, stay at home, and play drums?" This was what I wanted, and my mother had asked, but this did not go over so well.

Dad: "Hell no."

Me: "Why can't I?"

Dad: "I'll get arrested if you don't go to school."

Me: "Screw you. I don't care."

Mom: "Okay, let's all calm down. Mike, what would make you happy?"

Me: "I want to play drums all day because it's the only thing that makes me happy."

After a long pause, my mother said, "Give me a week to figure it out." They both went back into the house after that.

I am extremely impatient and was eager to know what she was up to. I asked her and she wouldn't tell me. This was incredibly frustrating.

Towards the end of the week, she sat me down to talk. She told me that I had an audition next week at the Long Island High School for the Arts.

Hearing this news was so exciting. If accepted, I would get what I wanted—to play drums all day, and without dropping out of school.

I immediately began practicing drums like an athlete training for the olympics, determined to give the best performance that I could at this audition.

A week later, my dad drove me to the audition, and we got to walk around the beautiful campus before my audition.

As we explored the Long Island High School for the Arts, I started to get nervous. I knew I had what it took to play at any level, but there was so much at stake. This single audition felt like it would determine my entire future.

Either I would get to play drums and grow as a drummer at this new school, or I would be forced to find an alternative high school to waste away in while dreaming of drumming each day.

Outside of one mistake, the audition went really well, and I was fairly confident that I had done enough to get in. A few days later, the director of the school's music department called my mom to tell her that I had been accepted.

I couldn't believe what my mother had pulled off. Not only was I amazingly happy that I could focus on drums and have a place where I belonged (a school for the arts), I once again had hope. As great as it was getting into this school, I had to split my time, spending half the day at the school for the arts and the other half at Uniondale High School. Still, I was too excited about my new school to mind traveling between schools.

I remember my first day at the Long Island High School for the Arts like it was yesterday. I walked in confidently with a huge afro, long bushy sideburns, and a t-shirt that said "GIRLS SUCK." I was surrounded with people just as unique as I was, and it felt great.

I even ran into one of my friends, Dwight, from Boy Scouts. It didn't take long to know that my last two years of high school were going to be special. The only thing I was hesitant about was spending half of each day back at Uniondale High School.

Uniondale High School was in the district where I had been expelled from elementary school in the fourth grade. Fortunately, having spent so many years in private schools, my reputation for bad behavior didn't follow me.

I'm not sure if my new teachers had a secret understanding with each other, all liked me, or just didn't care what I did, but they all went out of their way to give me passes to go down to the band room and play drums. So even though I was only in the school for the arts a few hours a day, I really did get to play drums all day, which was the best type of therapy I could possibly receive.

These two years changed my life and shaped what I would do after high school. My grades went up, medication went down, and the number of counseling sessions I needed each month were cut in half. I no longer had a problem attracting girls, and I even got a scholarship to Hofstra University. This gave me room to explore something that had been on my mind for awhile—religion.

As a junior in Uniondale High School, I wrote a paper on the commonalities amongst the three most popular religions: Judaism, Christianity, and Islam. Through my research, I started to throw out assumptions I had been taught at an early age and instead think deeper about what I actually believed in and why.

Through this research, I discovered that I connected the most with Eastern religion and meditation, and I began to adopt meditation into my daily routine. I wasn't actively trying to reject my faith, but found something that spoke to me and has contributed greatly to my happiness and success during this time and beyond.

As my drumming continued to improve and everything in my personal life was coming together, my teachers in both schools started to recommend me for paying gigs. Things were going so well that I was eventually taken off medication, and I stopped going to my psychiatrist. My parents were happy and supportive, but they were either skeptical or afraid of me continuing to pursue my dream of becoming a professional drummer.

Every time I got a new paid gig, they made comments about how these gigs wouldn't last and encouraged me to pursue a more stable career. They began pressuring me to become a music teacher, which I had no interest in other than the fact that I would occasionally get to play drums. It was hard for me to understand why my parents wanted me to do anything other than becoming a drummer when they knew it was the only thing in life I wanted and helped me keep my mental health in check.

After graduating from high school, I started school at Hofstra University as a music major. I balanced school and working as a professional drummer on the side. During the winter break of my freshman year, while most of classmates went home to meet up with old friends or take a part-time job at a local restaurant. I was flying to Texas to make a $1,000 playing a corporate gig.

As I continued to grow my drumming career, it started becoming hard to focus in college and take my professors seriously, especially when I knew that I was making more money than some of them were making. After five years attending college, I decided to quit and become a drummer full time.

It was a great move, and I was happy. For nearly a decade after, I rarely struggled to find work.

I played on two Broadway show karaoke albums; performed with a world-class drum band, The Hip Pickles; played with Nickelodeon's Dirty Sock Funtime Band; and worked with the staff composer of ABC's All My Children. Things were going really well in my career and my life. I was happy, busy, and living my dream of playing drums professionally, and I didn't expect it ever to end.

I was convinced that my mental health challenges of the past would stay in the past, and that depression, anxiety, self-harm, acting out, hospitalizations, and medications would no longer be part of my life. I was finally on my path to becoming a superhero, or so I thought.

This chapter covers life as a young adult and the beginning my career as a professional drummer. During this time, I learned that while my mental health challenges were difficult, the stigma surrounding the subject of mental health made those challenges even worse.

This understanding forever changed my life.

TRIGGER WARNING: This chapter contains a description of self-harm.

CHAPTER 6

COMING OUT OF THE CLOSET

I'd love to tell you that I lived happily ever after, and that I never had to worry about my mental health challenges again. Obviously, since you're reading my book on transforming the stigma around mental health, you know that's not true. But for the most part, my life after high school went well.

I had a steady, growing career; a healthy long-term relationship; and strong friendships. However, I struggled financially. Drumming professionally was rewarding and provided a decent pay. But getting paid and finding consistent work was difficult.

I often went weeks without knowing if I would be able to pay my bills or how I was going to have enough money to fix my car. I hate to tell you I was a "starving artist" but I didn't know a lot about the business side of being a self-employed artist, nor did I want to at the time.

I just wanted to play drums all day and get paid incredibly well for it. Was that too much to ask?

Because I never knew when I would get booked for a gig or when I would get paid for it, I was constantly stressed. My friends were all in stable careers, climbing up the corporate ladder. They were becoming successful while I was constantly worrying about cash flow.

Still, I was living a good life doing something I loved. In my spare time, I learned how to run a business through reading books that I purchased at a local bookstore.

I started to read a book a month. Then two books a month. And then a book every week.

In fact, I became addicted to books. I began picking up just about anything that sounded interesting, giving me a wide perspective on dozens of topics.

Reading these books gave me insight into how other people saw the world, different industries, and how people from all walks of life became successful. I believed that I could become this successful too.

Applying everything I read to my life wasn't quite as easy as reading about it. As much as I tried to change, my mental health held me back from growing forward. Starting the day I graduated high school, I experienced on-again off-again bouts of depression that lasted around a week at most.

They seemed to come out of nowhere, and I had a hard time realizing it was depression at the time. I just felt unmotivated, empty, and lazy.

I didn't want to do anything or talk to anyone, and withdrew from others. Most of my time was now spent alone. When people asked why I was isolating myself, I would make excuses.

In the summer, I blamed it on the humid Long Island weather. During other times of the year, I blamed it on other things like issues with women, not having any money, and being too busy with other aspects of my life.

I'm still not sure what caused these bouts and my desire to isolate from everyone, but once it was triggered, it had a snowball effect, and it kept rolling, getting bigger and bigger. The growing snowball slowly escalated into unhealthy behavior.

Instead of just keeping outbursts to myself and withdrawing, I acted out through passive aggressive temper tantrums that other people started to notice. During these tantrums, I would attack people verbally and emotionally. These were similar to what I experienced as a child.

As a kid, when these small episodes happened, my mother would always remind me that my psychiatrist, Dr. T, said this would happen from time to time, and it was ok. But that didn't bring me comfort at this point in my life. These tantrums made me feel like I wasn't good enough to be around others, causing me to withdraw even more.

On top of that, I worried how others viewed me socially. Acting out a little here or there could result in people recognizing signs of my mental health challenges. I didn't want to be judged.

While things in my life weren't perfect, I felt that any setback could ruin everything I worked so hard to get. Even going to a psychiatrist or counselor was out of the question because I thought it might jeopardize my career.

There were many times when the help of a mental health professional would have truly helped me, but I was afraid I would fail in life, and I was only interested in moving forward. This all changed in 2011.

I was five years into my relationship with Tara, and we were living together. We weren't soul mates, but we were comfortable with each other, which is more than I can say for my relationship with myself. Although Tara and I were comfortable in our relationship, we both started to feel pressure.

One of our friends got married, and then another, then another. I was off to a bachelor party one week and traveling out of state the next for a wedding. Even Jason, my younger brother, had gotten married and seemed a lot happier than I was.

I've never been one to give into the pressure from others; I usually fight it. But, I desperately wanted to be feel better. I knew that deep down I was in pain, and I thought that anything I could do to bridge that gap between pain and happiness was worth trying.

Thus, I figured getting married was an ideal solution. . After all, what could be better than deciding to get married because of pressure, stress, and depression? Those always work out, right?

Tara and I went on a trip to Las Vegas that summer. Flights were cheap, and we got a great deal on a hotel room for the week. The trip was short and not that much fun, yet, before our flight back, I put down a deposit for a wedding at the chapel at the Mandalay Bay Hotel to get married on the following Halloween.

I should've been happy and excited about our future and relieved that I made this decision. Instead, the pressure continued to build until I couldn't breathe. On the flight back home, 30,000 feet in the air, I felt trapped.

My heart was racing, hands were sweating, and my vision was blurry. I felt trapped being on the plane, but I also felt like I was trapped outside of my own body—like I was looking down at myself as a concerned third party.

"Please bring the plane down and get me help!" I screamed inside my head, but I held back my urge to demand that the flight attendant tell the pilot that this passenger wanted him or her to land the plane. I knew that if I couldn't control myself, my actions would get me arrested, if not worse.

After several hours of torture, the plane began its final descent for landing. I couldn't wait to walk off the plane, thinking it would bring the much needed relief from the pressure.

Once I stepped off of the plane, walked through the terminal, and into LaGuardia Airport in New York, nothing happened. There was no release. I felt no relief.

My first panic attack turned into my new reality for more than just a few hours. That night, I struggled to fall asleep, but finally drifted off in the early morning. When I woke up, I felt slightly better, but I had to work on holding back the Mike who could hardly get through a plane ride without requesting an emergency landing.

Over the next several days, I felt happy one minute, sad the next, and angry soon after. Tara, trying to help, suggested that I see a therapist.

"You're my issue; maybe you should get help for yourself," I snapped back. I was going to deny that I had a problem at all costs. I stormed out of the apartment, got into my car, and started to drive.

This drive was a bumpy one. As I drove east on the Grand Central Parkway, my anger and anxiety were moving faster than I could drive my little Honda. I soon could no longer see or think clearly enough to stay on the road. I pulled off to the shoulder by Mitchell Air Force Base in Garden City, New York.

For two hours, I tried to sit still and calm down, but I just couldn't. My chest was tight, and my entire body tingled uncomfortably.

I was scared, angry, and sad at different moments, and I couldn't sort things out or come down from this awful, anxious peak. I felt like I was on top of a mountain without any equipment or knowledge on how to get back down safely.

However, I wasn't ready to give up yet. I continued to breathe deeply, trying to calm down. While I couldn't come all the way down off my mountain of stress and worry, I was confident enough that I could resume driving, so I got back behind the wheel and was on my way.

I drove wherever the road would take me with no plans of stopping. Back at home, Tara, not knowing what to do, called the police.

I just wanted a way out of this mess. I wanted my thoughts, emotional pain, and physical pain, and the frustration that came with it, to stop. I decided I needed to die.

Unlike my fifth-grade overdose, this time, I would make sure that I followed through. I could no longer rely on therapy or pills to heal my pain. But I wasn't sure how I would die.

I could stop the car in the middle of a railroad crossing. I could jump off a building—they were easy to find in New York. I could poison myself or buy a gun and end it quickly.

Being so overwhelmed with worry and flooded with thoughts and emotions, I couldn't make a firm decision, other than knowing

I wanted to die. Knowing the police were likely at my apartment, I couldn't go back there even if I wanted to. I knew from past experience what would happen if the police got involved, and the last thing I wanted was to end up in jail or back in a mental hospital.

I pulled off the highway in Roslyn, New York. I still didn't know exactly where I was going, but I did know why and what I was going to do when I got there. I found a small drug store, walked in, and made a single purchase: a box of razor blades.

After that, I sat in the parking lot of the drugstore inside my car, and began self-harming with the razor blades. At the time, self-harming helped ease my pain because I didn't know a better way to deal with it and was too scared and stubborn to get the help I needed.

It's hard to explain how I felt. I felt both aware and unaware at the same time, and after awhile I just stopped self-harming. I sat there bleeding, staring out my driver's side window.

This whole ordeal left me tired, both physically and emotionally. I wanted the pain to go away, but I also just wanted to sleep. I put the razor blades away and headed home.

After walking in the door around midnight, I found Tara upset, worried, and anxious, but she let me go to bed. She wanted to help me, but didn't know how.

I left her in a tough position because I wouldn't get help for myself. If she pushed me too hard, there was no telling how I would react. If she didn't try at all, I would never get the help I needed.

In the days that followed, I developed a pattern. I would go to sleep, wake up in a zombie-like state, get in my car, and just drive. I would eventually come home and start the cycle over again.

When I drove, I would sometimes go to Long Beach, which has

always been a calming place for me. Other times I would go to my favorite coffee shops and just hang out for hours at a time. And sometimes I would drive wherever the road would take me.

After a couple of weeks, both Tara and I grew exhausted of my constant outbursts, shifting moods, and constant self-harm. But I didn't know where or how to find the help I needed?

I looked through my contacts in my phone to see if I knew of anyone who could help me out. Fortunately, I found someone: Cheryl Williams. I met Cheryl a few years before my mental health exploded and my life was trending towards its darkest moments. I was leading drumming workshops for youth with mental health challenges.

Cheryl was friendly, and having seen me at my best, I thought she would be someone who could understand the dire situation I was now in and help me get the emergency help I needed.

"Hi Cheryl, this is Mike Veny."

"Hello, Mike! It's so good to hear from you. How are you?"

Cheryl is one of those people you meet who actually means it when they ask you how you're doing. I told her the truth. I explained that I was harming myself, couldn't control my emotions, and was on the verge of ending my life.

"There's an upcoming children's mental health event that I'm hosting. Can you be my keynote speaker?" she asked.

I was stunned.

"Are you kidding? Did you hear what I said? Absolutely not. I need help. Is there anyone you can refer me to?"

However, since Cheryl doesn't give up on something she is determined to do without a fight, she said, "Mike, this would be a great fit! We would love to have you speak, and you could bring a lot to the kids at the event. Picture it—Mike Veny, drummer and mental health speaker."

In response, I ended the call politely. I needed help, and instead she tried to talk me into speaking to kids about mental health, which was the last thing I wanted to do.

I woke up the next day, still trying to figure out how I would get the help I needed, and went through my normal daily routine. I took a shower, ate breakfast, and opened up my laptop to check my emails.

Looking through my email inbox, I didn't know if I should be outraged or impressed with what I saw. There was an email from Cheryl: a formal invitation to speak at the children's mental health event I had refused the previous day. She sent a copy of this email to people from the New York State Office of Mental Health and several other people who knew me.

I sat there and just stared at the screen. I wanted to be angry, but I had to admire her persistence. Still, the thought of speaking publicly about mental health challenges seemed ridiculous to me.

As a professional drummer, I was comfortable speaking about music or the music business because I had achieved a certain level of success and had real-world knowledge of the topic.

But with my own mental health, I felt like a complete failure. Who was I to lead others in a discussion about mental health?

I knew she wasn't going to give up easily, so I decided to put real thought into giving this speech. I made a list of pros and cons.

Pros:

- By doing this event, I would have to stay alive until the event happened.

- Speakers get paid.
- This would give me an opportunity to talk about my challenges and maybe make me feel better.
- I knew that there were other people like me, struggling with the same kind of pain that I was struggling with. Maybe I could help someone else even if I couldn't help myself.

Cons:

- I was ashamed of where I was at mentally.
- I had no idea what to say.
- I could embarrass myself and make my challenges worse.

After some serious reflection, the pros outweighed the cons. I asked her how much they would pay me, and she said $500.

It wasn't a lot compared to what I thought public speakers made for a speech, but it was more than I made during most of my performances as a drummer. I told her to count me in; now I just had to figure out what to say. Luckily, I had some time to figure it out

Outside of my new professional opportunity, I had other new experiences: I followed through on my down payment and got married on Halloween. Deep down inside, I knew getting married was a mistake, but I did it anyway.

I thought, like many other people, that some of my problems and the pressure I felt would go away, or at least get a little bit better, by getting married. It hadn't gone away, and it wasn't getting any better.

Shortly after we tied the knot, we both knew it was over, but we dragged it out waiting for something magical to save our marriage. I was also battling the intensity of my own mental health challenges, which weren't getting better.

To avoid thinking about my bad decision, I spent a lot of time reflecting, thinking what I would say during my upcoming speech. I felt like every bad thing in our marriage was my fault, and that burden became too great for me to carry. Fortunately, our separation played out more like a conversation among business partners deciding to go their separate ways than a messy divorce.

While still in the midst of a marriage that I knew wasn't going to work and dealing with escalating emotional challenges, I started actively looking for a therapist. It couldn't be that hard, right? All you had to do is go find one on the internet, schedule an appointment, and you were in.

Wrong. Surprisingly, at least for me in New York City, this was a much more difficult process than I had ever imagined. I made call after call without any response for weeks.

When I did hear back, it was the same story each time:"We'd love to have you come in. We can see you in about six weeks, will that work?"

I knew that I needed help and was ready to get started, but it I couldn't find a therapist.

After rehearsal with a band one night in New York City, I left the room and got into an elevator. It was one of those really small, old elevators that looked like something out of a movie, and not a romantic comedy, more like a suspense thriller where people disappeared never to be seen again after entering the cramped death trap. It was small, wooden, and poorly lit.

Additionally, it was very slow and didn't seem to ever land level with the floor. But I made the fateful decision to step into the elevator, and it changed my life forever.

A few seconds later, a woman walked into the elevator with me. I consider myself good at picking up people's energy, and she had a warm energy.

Maybe it was my anxiety, my natural flirtatiousness, or maybe it was something else, but I decided to have a conversation with her. Hey, if we were going to be stuck together in the tiny elevator of death we might as well be friendly, right?

I said hello, and she responded back, "Hello." I then told her that I felt that this building was a little sketchy, hoping she would laugh. She responded by smiling and letting me know that she worked there.

I decided to take our conversation a step further. "What kind of work do you do??" I asked. "I'm a therapist," she responded.

Without missing a beat, I said, "Oh, I'm mentally ill. May I have your business card?" She gave me her card, and has been my therapist ever since.

I felt a bit better knowing that I now had someone to talk to about my challenges. I also had a speaking engagement to look forward to.

As I thought about what I wanted to say in my speech, I spent time reflecting on my life, which felt like an entire lifetime of struggling with depression, anger, anxiety, and obsession. The thought of having to go through this for the rest of my life was daunting and demoralizing. I was so ashamed of who I was that I didn't want other people to know about my history, which left me feeling alone and isolated.

These feelings were the effects of the stigma surrounding mental health. I also realized that if I was experiencing it, I wasn't alone. As I began to dig further into learning about mental health, I found an interesting trend: mental health was becoming an increasingly popular topic to discuss in our society, but at the same time, *people were reluctant to talk about it.*

There were also people who needed treatment for more severe mental health challenges than I had, and they weren't getting it. This realization shifted my focus from my own mental health challenges to how I could help others.

Two months before my speech, Cheryl called me. She asked if I could do another speech in for another group that she was affiliated with a few days before speaking at her event. By doing this talk, I could get more experience talking about mental health in front of an audience and work in something I was comfortable with— drumming.

The big day finally came, and I felt ready to make first speech. I walked up to the podium with a sheet of notes and left in tears to a standing ovation.

After the talk, I was flooded by people who wanted to talk to me about their own mental health challenges. With a simple speech, a subject that's normally taboo suddenly became something that everyone in the room wanted to discuss openly.

A few days later I arrived at the event Cheryl initially hired me for. Although I gave a speech just a few days before, I felt nervous. In my speech, I talked about my experiences as a child and how misunderstood I was, and how I know that there were millions of other people out there just like me.

As I talked about my experience in high school, I was overcome with emotion, and I cried again, which was just the second time I had ever cried as an adult. I finished my speech, and after a couple of tense and silent seconds, I received another standing ovation.

It was at this moment that I knew the direction my life would take. Whether or not I liked it, my purpose was to empower mental wellness.

This wasn't because of the standing ovations, but because of the feeling that came from the process of speaking publicly about my own mental health. It was therapy that paid me and had the potential to help others. Based on the feedback I received from these presentations, just talking about my experiences inspired others to begin talking more openly about this sensitive subject.

By the end of the year, I was flying around the country making speeches about the stigma surrounding mental health to audiences ranging from school children to corporations. My life began to have new meaning. I was discovering what it meant to be a mental wellness superhero.

PART 2

UNDERSTANDING STIGMA

Every superhero has a cause that they fight for. In this chapter, you will learn about the stigma surrounding mental health and how it affects everyone. Before you begin your mission to save the world, it's important that you understand the problem.

As you read, keep in mind that you or someone you know is being affected by this right now, whether you realize it or not. Everyone experiences pain, but no one needs to suffer.

CHAPTER 7

DEFINING STIGMA

Several years after my first presentation about mental health, I presented at a state youth conference. The presentation went well, and towards the end of it, I took questions from the audience.

At this particular event, I was asked something I had never been asked before: "What is 'mental health' exactly?" I thought it was a silly question. I assumed that everyone knew what the term "mental health" meant.

Pausing to think about his question, I responded with the best answer I could. "I'm not really sure... brain health, I guess," I said with uncertainty. Her question helped me realize that not only could I not explain the term to others, but I also didn't have a precise definition for myself. This was embarrassing.

With the stigma surrounding mental health, and other stigmas in life, when we don't have a basic understanding of the subject, it actually increases the stigma and damages efforts to transform it for the better. Her question stayed with me long after the conference was over. In pursuit of a clear answer for myself, I began researching the term "mental health" online and quickly discovered a wide variety of definitions.

No wonder people don't understand what it means—not even professionals can agree on a definition. And when there's confusion around what something is, like mental health, it prevents and misleads people from wanting to learn about it and getting help for themselves and others. I decided to make it my mission to come up with a clear definition I was comfortable with and others could clearly understand.

The World Health Organization defines mental health as "a state of well-being in which every individual realizes his or her own potential, can cope with the normal stresses of life, can work productively and fruitfully, and is able to make a contribution to her or his community."[6]

Mental health is invisible except for what you can observe in a person's behavior, bloodwork, or brain scans. Although the above definition is complete in my opinion, there's an inherent confusion that lies in the word "mental." In Merriam-Webster's Dictionary, the first listed definition of the word "mental" is "of or relating to the mind."[7]

---

6 "Mental health: a state of well-being." WHO. Accessed December 2017. http://www.who.int/features/factfiles/mental_health/en/.

7 Merriam-Webster, s.v. "mental," accessed December 2017. https://www. merriam-webster.com/dictionary/mental

This leads us to conclude that "mental health" is mainly about "thought health." But in my experience, mental health goes much deeper than just the health of our thoughts.

For example, I know that when I'm not mentally healthy I am thinking negative thoughts that spiral out of control quickly. My feelings are like a nonstop roller coaster throughout the day—going up, down, and upside down. I act inappropriately towards myself and other people in my life.

It was at that moment that I realized that my thoughts, feelings, and behaviors are a part of what we have come to refer to as "mental health." The root of mental health all starts with thoughts. Thoughts impact feelings. Your feelings impact your behavior. Your behaviors affect your thoughts, for better or for worse.

As Mahatma Ghandi once said, *"Your beliefs become your thoughts, your thoughts become your words, your words become your actions, your actions become your habits, your habits become your values, your values become your destiny."* If left uncared for, each will continue to disrupt the others. But this cycle can be play out positively when negative thoughts and feelings are dealt with appropriately.

Stigma is defined as "a set of negative and often unfair beliefs that a society or group of people have about something."[8] There are many unfair beliefs when it comes to how we all think of others with mental health challenges, from thinking they have the potential to be violent to thinking that having mental health challenges is a weakness or character flaw. Stigma can exist around any subject, but we will focus on how stigma impacts mental health.

"Stigmatizing attitudes are not limited to mental illness. Persons with physical illness and disabilities are also the object of disparaging opin-

---

8 Merriam-Webster, s.v. "stigma," accessed December 2017. https://www.merriam-webster.com/dictionary/stigma

ion. However, the general public seems to disapprove of persons with severe mental illness significantly more than persons with physical disabilities." [9]

Stigma typically includes the following:

1. **Stereotypes:** "to believe unfairly that all people or things with a particular characteristic are the same."

2. **Prejudice:** "an unfair feeling of dislike for a person or group because of race, sex, religion, etc."or "a feeling of like or dislike for someone or something especially when it is not reasonable or logical"

3. **Discrimination:** "the practice of unfairly treating a person or group of people differently from other people or groups of people" or "the ability to recognize the difference between things that are of good quality and those that are not" or "the ability to understand that one thing is different from another thing."[10]

In summary, stereotypes are related to **thoughts**; prejudice comes from **feelings**; discrimination relates to a person's **behavior**. Stigma, just like my definition of the phrase "mental health," impacts our thoughts, feelings, and behaviors. So how can the same ingredients that contribute negatively to the growing stigma around mental health be the same that establish and maintain our mental health?

While I don't believe there is a strong conclusion as to why they have the same ingredients, it's clear that stereotypes, prejudice,

---

9 Patrick W. Corrigan., David Roe, and Hector W. H. Stang. *Challenging the stigma of mental illness: lessons for therapists and advocates.* Chichester, West Sussex, UK: John Wiley & Sons, 2011.

10 Stephen P. Henshaw. *The mark of shame: stigma of mental illness and an agenda for change.* New York, NY: Oxford University Press, 2010.

and discrimination have a negative impact on our mental health. Stigma is not only unhealthy for the people with a medical condition or disability, it's unhealthy for the person who believes it. If you believe that someone may become violent at any given time because they have a mental health challenge, they may keep themselves away or act aggressively towards you in an effort to defend themselves.

This can be a lot to understand without tangible data. Thanks to mental health advocates and organizations, we have proof that stigma impacts people who battle with or are perceived to battle with mental health challenges.

In a 2007 survey of adults who showed symptoms of mental health challenges, "only 25% believed that people are caring and sympathetic to people with mental illness."[11] Most likely, the majority of that 75%, people struggling with mental health and not believing others will respect their ailment without judgment, will avoid disclosing their challenges at all costs.

This is where stigma impacts those with mental health challenges. Whether they are right or not, the belief that others won't be sympathetic towards their mental health challenges hurts their ability to receive treatment and emotional support.

"The threat of stigma, and the effort to avoid the label, are so powerful that more than half of the people with mental illness who would probably benefit from psychiatric services never obtain even an initial interview with a professional. Stigma is personal." [12]

As a person with mental health challenges, I've always believed

---

11   "Stigma of Mental Illness." Centers for Disease Control and Prevention. October 04, 2013. Accessed December 2017. https://www.cdc.gov/mentalhealth/data_stats/mental-illness.htm.

12   Corrigan, Roe, Stang, *Challenging the Stigma*

that some people were not caring and sympathetic towards people like me. I have lived in fear of what would happen when people "found out."

I avoided conversations about mental health and steered discussions in different directions when they were starting to get into topics surrounding mental health, leading to feeling like I lived a double life and couldn't be myself.

With no surety that people will be sympathetic and understanding, it's hard to know how they will react when you tell them you've been diagnosed with Bipolar disorder or that you live with Obsessive-Compulsive Disorder (OCD). And if you don't know how they will react, how can you feel comfortable sharing? No one wants to be condemned or laughed at by someone they know or even by a stranger.

Sometimes, I felt ashamed for having mental health challenges. Other times, I felt like my mental health challenges were a part of my past, and I wasn't one of "those people" anymore.

Sometimes, I felt like I didn't have mental health challenges at all. Occasionally, I even joined in on talking badly about people who struggled with their own mental health challenges to steer people away from my own challenges.

In his books *The Mark of Shame: Stigma of Mental Illness and an Agenda for Change*, author Stephen Hinshaw explains how stigma affects those who are living with mental health challenges. "People with mental illness still continue to suffer discrimination, including a lack of viable opportunities for housing and employment, as well as restrictions on the right to vote, obtain a driver's license, or maintain child custody."[13]

---

13   Henshaw, The *Mark of Shame*

The National Alliance on Mental Illness (NAMI) also provides insight on the devastating impact of stigma. "Discrimination against people who have mental illnesses keeps them from seeking help. While one in five Americans live with a mental disorder, estimates indicate that nearly two-thirds of all people with a diagnosable mental illness do not seek treatment, especially people from diverse communities, because they lack the knowledge or they fear disclosure, rejection of friends, and discrimination. Discrimination against people with mental illness violates their rights and denies them opportunities. Despite Civil Rights Law such as the Americans with Disabilities Act, people with mental illnesses often experience discrimination in the workplace, education, housing, and healthcare."

NAMI states that stigma leads to:

- Inadequate insurance coverage for mental health services
- Fear, mistrust, and violence against people living with mental illness and their families
- Family and friends turning their backs on people with mental illness
- Prejudice and discrimination

Just look at how the subject of mental health has been portrayed in music, movies, and television. One of my favorite childhood cartoons *Animaniacs* features Yacko, Wacko, and Dot —three "crazy" siblings. They were locked away in a water tower and subjected to treatments and experiments that didn't work. To some effect, they made being "crazy" cool, but they also further perpetuated stereotypes.

The effect of stigma on those who could benefit from treatment is devastating, and is something that needs to change. With nearly 66% of people with diagnosable mental health challenges not seeking out treatment, our society is suffering from stigma, and people are not able to live their lives to the fullest.

Stigma is often worse than mental health challenges themselves. Because of the stigma surrounding mental health, people don't feel comfortable discussing it with others, preventing them from getting the help they needed to be their best self. Even in places where we should be comfortable to share anything, like churches and social groups, people with mental challenges are seen as "having demons" or as someone to avoid.

Stigma breaks up relationships, ends jobs, destroys families, and ruins lives. It serves as a dirty rumor that grows and grows until it's so big no one really cares if it's true or not, and it demolishes everything in its path.

"Stigma is both a subtle and broadly felt experience." [14]

But there is hope.

My first speaking engagement gave me something to look forward to. As I thought about what I wanted to say, I spent time reflecting on my life.

It felt like a lifetime of struggling with depression, anger, anxiety, and obsessing. I was frustrated. These challenges had taken a toll on my self esteem and self confidence. I wanted to get rid of them and the same time I knew that I was stuck with them for life.

This made me feel so angry! The thought of having to go through this for the rest of my life was daunting and demoralizing.

- I was ashamed of who I was.

14   Corrigan, Roe, Stang, *Challenging the Stigma*

- I didn't want other people to know about my history.
- I felt alone and isolated.

That is what I thought. Here's what I now know:

"Only by understanding stigma can we hope to beat it." [15]

15   Corrigan, Roe, Stang, *Challenging the Stigma*

As you begin to have a better understanding of stigma, it's essential to explore how it originates and continues to develop. Your awareness of this is critical to Transforming Stigma™.

This chapter will introduce you to a new paradigm. This paradigm is the foundation for your development as mental wellness superhero.

CHAPTER 8

THE STIGMA CYCLE™

As we dig deeper into this problem, we need to understand the Law of the Tribe, along with the the Law of Confusion and Frustration, and how they play a role in The Stigma Cycle™.

The Law of the Tribe

We are tribal people by nature and everyone wants to be part of groups—even those people who say they hate people.

We learn about socializing in groups from a very early age. You can observe this in kindergarten classrooms throughout the United States.

The way people develop relationships is by finding out what they have in common with one another. For example, a group of three kindergarten students are socializing.

1. Student 1 & Student 2 have the same pair of sneakers
2. Student 3 has a different pair of sneakers.
3. Students 1 & 2 now label Student 3 as "weird"

Children figure out who the weird one is because it's a way of knowing who isn't in the group. If you aren't weird, you're in. If you are weird, you aren't.

We continue to practice this law throughout our lives. As adults, nobody wants to be the weird one. In my opinion, this is one of the reasons for the stigma surrounding mental health.

Since the beginning of time, people who experienced mental health challenges were labeled as weird, demonic, or below other people.

The Law of Confusion and Frustration

Mental health challenges are confusing and frustrating.

They are confusing for those that experience them and people who observe someone experiencing them. That's why it's so hard for people to understand.

Unlike other medical issues, mental health challenges don't often reveal themselves immediately. They are eventually uncovered through behavior patterns and a crisis.

One morning I was doing challenging push ups in the gym. On every single rep, I had to push my bodyweight up fast so my hands came off the floor, changed hand positions, and then came back down.

OUCH!

I felt a sharp pain in my wrist. I immediately stopped exercising, went into the locker room and changed clothes, and headed home. My wrist continued to hurt, and I was eager to get home to put ice on it.

The pain was clear, and if it didn't heal in a day or so, I would call a doctor. It was either a sprain, strain, or a broken wrist.

When it comes to mental health challenges, they don't identify themselves so clearly. Most people don't wake up and say, "I feel depressed today. I should make an appointment to see a therapist."

It's only after a period of time showing problematic behavior, that they start to realize that something much deeper is going on. For example, one might experience difficulty performing at work, not taking care of personal hygiene, etc., before that person may even CONSIDER they are struggling with a mental health challenge.

And even if they do consider it, there is often shame in seeking help.

On the flip side, I remember when I was a child and my mom told that one of my uncles was "mentally ill". I remember the tone she used and knew on an emotional level that mental health challenges were a bad thing.

This particular uncle didn't seem much different than the other adults, but as I began to observe his behavior, it appeared as though something was off. It was frustrating because I couldn't make sense of it. It was confusing.

The Law of the Tribe and the Law of Confusion affect people who are struggling with mental health challenges and their loved ones.

These laws offer you some insight into how the the phrase "mental health" has such a negative connotation. This negative connotation leads to feelings of shame, silence, and isolation among people who live with mental health challenges and their loved ones. *Sadly, it prevents people who are struggling from getting the help that they need.*

This is The Stigma Cycle™

As I began to dig further into the subject, I came to the conclusion that when people use the term "stigma" they aren't actually referring to the definition: a mark of shame. They are referring to a cycle that begins with shame. The cycle happens as follows:

1. Stigma starts with shame.

2. Shame leads to silence.

3. Silence leads to sabotage, self-destructive behavior, social injustice, and suicide.

4. The cycle then repeats itself.

Here's how **The Stigma Cycle™** works for someone, like myself, who is living with a mental health challenge:

1. I feel ashamed because of my challenges. I have had them my whole entire life and it's a burden.

2. I don't talk about them. I don't want anyone to know about them.

3. I isolate myself, self-harm, display suicidal tendencies, and my condition gets worse.

4. As it gets worse, I feel even more shame and the cycle repeats itself.

And so on...

Here's how **The Stigma Cycle™** works for a loved one of someone living with a mental health challenge:

1. They feel ashamed about the person's behavior patterns.

2. They don't talk about their struggle with this shame.

3. This leads to them developing their own mental health challenges AND their loved one not getting the help they need.

4. As it gets worse, they feel even more shame and the cycle repeats itself.

And so on...

Once this cycle began to make sense to me, I started to see how its been affecting me for my entire life. Although my mental health challenges were a burden, the stigma was even more of a burden.

This clarity gave me a new level of motivation and determination. While I was pretty certain that my depression and anxiety were here to stay and out of my control, the stigma was something I could control.

God grant me the serenity
to accept the things I cannot change;
courage to change the things I can;
and wisdom to know the difference.

— Reinhold Niebuhr

So I set out on a mission to transform stigma into strength. I knew it was possible but I didn't know how. I tried many different things and failed but eventually discovered some profound insights that brought about three dramatic changes in my life:

1. I started to feel less shame about my mental health challenges. In fact, I started to feel like they were part of what makes me special... even sexy.

2. I became comfortable talking to people about my past struggles and current recovery.

3. Other people began openly talking to me about their mental health challenges.

AND IT FELT GREAT!!!!

Feeling excited, I began sharing what I learned with others, driven to get this information to the entire world. I was amazed at the positive results other people and organizations began to experience with this knowledge.

A culture of Transforming Stigma™ into strength was beginning!

In the following chapters, I will share these insights with you in more detail. They are the "how to" of becoming a mental wellness superhero.

PART 3

TRANSFORMING STIGMA™ INTO STRENGTH

We are a success-oriented society. We want to win at life. We associate mental health challenges with weakness and failure since having "challenges" goes against the image most of us want to represent.

Stigma starts with shame. In this chapter, you will learn your first lesson in Transforming Stigma™ as a mental wellness superhero.

CHAPTER 9

TRANSFORMING SHAME

"I define shame as the intensely painful feeling or experience of believing that we are flawed and therefore unworthy of love and belonging something we've experienced, done, or failed to do makes us unworthy of connection.

I don't believe shame is helpful or productive. In fact, I think shame is much more likely to be the source of destructive, hurtful behavior than the solution or cure. I think the fear of disconnection can make us dangerous."[16]

So how do you transform shame?

---

16   Brene Brown. "Shame Versus Guilt." Accessed December 2017. https://brenebrown.com/blog/2013/01/14/shame-v-guilt/.

The key to understanding shame is to think about the opposite: pride and honor. And how do you get to a place of pride and honor? The answer is self-care.

Imagine you're sick with the flu, or at least that's what you think you have. After several days of being unable to eat, you decide to go to the doctor. The waiting room is busy, and you've been waiting for two hours. Finally, a male nurse comes into the waiting room and calls your name.

He takes you down several hallways to the front of a room with an old wooden door. You walk inside and climb up on the cold metal table. Thirty minutes later, your doctor comes in, and you begin to feel a sense of relief that you will finally get the help you need and start recovering from whatever it is you have.

As the doctor is asking you questions and checking out your symptoms, you start to smell something rotten. You look up at the doctor and see that his eyes are red, he's mumbling instead of speaking clearly, and the jacket he's wearing looks dirty and wrinkled.

"How are you doing, Doc?" you ask nervously. "Just looking forward to going home after 24 straight hours on the job; how about you?" Your sense of calm has gone away, and you now begin to wonder if this doctor is in the best position to give you proper care.

Would you trust this doctor, who is tired, smelly, and ready to go home, to make the right decisions about your care?

Now put yourself in your doctor's shoes. Are you your best self when you're tired, hungry, or uncared for?

When we're not at our best, we can't give our best to others or ourselves. Not only is your doctor not at his very best after working 24-hours straight, he also may have a hard time driving home, having conversations with others, and performing normal everyday tasks. In that moment, he is not taking care of himself, and that directly impacts his thoughts, feelings, and behaviors.

The moment you begin taking care of yourself, I begin to feel better about yourself and more confident in my superhero abilities. All superheroes have weaknesses. When they are not well rested, eating healthy, and in great shape, they are especially weak and vulnerable.

Unfortunately, few of us make self-care a priority. Despite the importance of taking care of ourselves, we just don't do it. According to the National Center for Biotechnology Information, only 6.6 percent of Americans with health conditions, ages 25 and older, practice self-care on a daily basis.[17] When self-care is not a priority, it can make any condition worse, and life in general becomes much harder to enjoy.

"Self-care is crucial," says Krystal Reddick in *Self-Care as Revolutionary Action*. "It is critical for your mental and physical health. And it is critical for stress management." [18]

You, as a Transforming Stigma™ superhero, have to take care of yourself in order to be at your best. This is the foundation for helping yourself and others. Whether you're transforming the stigma that you or someone else experiences, it begins with self-care. Addressing your own mental health needs is taking a stand against

17   Jonas, D. E., Y. Ibuka, and L. B. Russell. "How Much Time Do Adults Spend on Health-related Self-care? Results from the American Time Use Survey." The Journal of the American Board of Family Medicine 24, no. 4 (2011): 380-90. Accessed December 2017. doi:10.3122/jabfm.2011.04.100260.

18   Krystal Reddick "Self-Care as Revolutionary Action." January 6, 2015. Accessed December 2017. https://www.huffingtonpost.com/krystal-reddick/selfcare-as-revolutionary_b_6393154.html.

stigma. It's telling the world that what they think about you won't control your physical and mental health.

But before we can create a plan to take better care of ourselves, we need to discuss why we aren't taking care of ourselves.

In Stephen R. Covey's *The 7 Habits of Highly Effective People*, Covey discusses the difference between urgent and important activities. We place urgent activities ahead of important activities, which leads to us finding excuses to not address many of the things we feel are important, but are not urgent.

For example, exercise is important, but it often takes a backseat to the things that we deem to be urgent, like work or the needs of other people in our lives. Because we prioritize things that we feel are urgent, we don't make enough time for things that are important until they become urgent, and often it's too late, like a heart attack or a mental health breakdown.[19]

It's important to understand the difference between self-care activities and escape activities. Escape activities include watching television, engaging in social media, and substance abuse.

Although you may feel like you are practicing self-care when engaging in them, you actually aren't. Self-care activities, on the other hand, are intentional and proactive activities that help you grow as a person.

It's become acceptable to neglect ourselves and our own mental health care in order to address other aspects of our lives. If you called in sick to work tomorrow, your boss would most likely be understanding. But if you called in to tell your boss that you needed to take a mental health day, the reaction you'd get may not be as supportive.

---

19   Stephen R. Covey. The 7 habits of highly effective people: powerful lessons in personal change. New York: Free Press, 2014.

You may even be told to come in anyways or your boss might wonder if you are still mentally fit for your job. We talk about how many hours we worked this week instead of how much time we spent reading a book or meditating.

Additionally, we don't take the time to care for ourselves because we don't understand the benefits for it. We see self-care as an un-necessary and time-wasting burden that we'll just put off until we have more time. That "more time" never comes because we con-tinue, day after day and week after week, to place what we deem urgent at the top of our to-do list ahead of the many important things in our lives.

We think of tasks in terms of efficiency instead of effectiveness. Not all tasks can be efficient, but that doesn't mean they're not ef-fective. Taking care of yourself takes time, but it's worth the invest-ment.

Self-care leads to a better version of ourselves, which allows us to care for ourselves and others better. It gives us our superhe-ro-like powers and minimizes our weaknesses.

So how do we get started?

With anything in life, to make progress, you have to take a first step. With self-care, the first step is discovering what it takes for you to be both physically and mentally healthy. For me, taking care of myself includes five things:

- Exercise

- Playing drums

- Attending a mental health support group

- Surrounding myself with positive people

- Meditation

These five activities impact both my physical and mental well-being for the better. Exercise, for example, helps me get in better physical shape, and the positive impact it has on my brain and body makes me feel better emotionally. Meditation helps me connect with my higher power and gives my mind a break from the constant worries and stresses of life.

After knowing what activities are needed for you to take care of yourself, you have to work them into your everyday life. Creating some kind of consistency through a routine helps ground you and keeps your stress level manageable.

After reading *What the Most Successful People Do Before Breakfast: A Short Guide to Making Over Your Mornings – and Life*, I learned that having a consistent morning routine that starts at 6:30 a.m. (or before) is critical to success. I began engineering my morning routine this way.

Specifically, I wanted to take advantage of the first 30 minutes of my day since what happens in that time sets the tone for my entire day.

While working to reshape my mornings, a friend suggested reading Hal Elrod's book, *The Miracle Morning: The Not-So-Obvious Secret Guaranteed to Transform Your Life (Before 8AM)*. In the book, Hal use the acronym "SAVERS" to outline six actions to take each morning. SAVERS is an acronym for Silence, Affirmations, Visualization, Exercise, Reading, and Scribing (writing).

Here are ways that I've applied each:

Silence

For 30 minutes, I meditate each morning. As my meditation teacher taught me, meditation is a gift that you give yourself, and it helps keep you grounded.

Affirmations

It may feel silly to talk to yourself out loud, but affirmations can boost your confidence and affirm what you already know about yourself. I have five affirmations I say to myself each morning. These were created around specific habits and ways of thinking that I am cultivating within myself. I typically say in my affirmations in the first, second and third-person. For example, when I was doing affirmations to improve my self-esteem, I would say "I love me" a few times in the first-person; then in the second-person, "I love Michael. I love Michael. I love Michael;" and then third-person, "I love you. I love you. I love you."

Visualization

Can you picture yourself accomplishing what you want to accomplish? I mentally rehearse positive outcomes. Maybe it's a situation I have to confront or a chapter I need to finish writing. Regardless of what it is, I visualize a positive outcome. This helps me see what I want to accomplish, and I play out how this ideal scenario will become a reality.

Exercise

A weight training workout or brisk walk gets my body moving and heart rate up to start my day. When I'm traveling, I make it a point to go for walks, and I even travel with resistance rubber bands so I can do workouts in my hotel room. I also listen to good music and affirmation audio recordings to help my body and mind while exercising.

Reading

I read each morning, from a few pages of a book I'm trying to get through or an article in a magazine. I live by this mantra: leaders read and readers lead. I often read to help me tackle specific problems that I'm dealing with internally.

Scribing

Scribing is also known as writing. For my morning writing, I write down what's on my mind and what I have to get done that day or I write in my gratitude journal. Writing in my gratitude journal helps remind myself what's good in my life.

While I'm not perfect in always following my morning routine, I try my hardest to stick to it each day. Even if I only do half of the things that I just shared, it puts me in a much better place mentally, and I actually feel much better about myself regardless of the challenges that I might be facing.

The moment me eyes open in the morning, my objective is to start my day with RPM— rise, pee, and meditate. Right before I start meditating, I grab a glass of iced water with lemon and take my antidepressant medication.

Since I began practicing these "Life SAVERS," I can honestly say that I have felt happier, been less stressed, and been more productive than ever before. Most importantly, I have been more present for the important people and activities in my life. By taking a little extra time in the morning, I now have better days and a healthier, happier me.

After creating a healthier routine, my focus switched to keeping this routine consistent. I didn't want to fall back into my bad habits. Self-care is more than just a morning routine—It's a completely new and better way to approach life. It includes consistent work in four areas of our lives:

- Spiritual

- Mental

- Physical

- Social-Emotional

Maslow's Hierarchy of needs describes the basic necessities in each of those areas. At the bottom, we have our basic physical needs—food and water—then we have our basic mental needs—safety and belonging—next, is the basic social-emotional needs—intimate relationships, friends, and feelings of accomplishment—at the top is the basic spiritual needs—achieving one's full potential.

As stated our **spiritual** journey comes from an innate need to grow, succeed in life, and live the best life possible. This is why making time for spirituality is important.

For me, I tend to lean towards Eastern religions for spiritual wisdom and guidance, particularly through meditation. I'm a big believer in meditation, which has been key in my recovery and the recovery of others living with mental health challenges.

On a physical level, meditation relaxes me and relieves my stress. On a mental level, it calms my mind. On a social and emotional level, it makes me more present and aware of my feelings. On a spiritual level, it connects me to my higher power.

Each day, I try to meditate for 30 minutes. It's the most precious time during my day because I get to relax and connect with my higher power.

After meditating, I find that no matter what else is going on in my life, I have a feeling of peace, wholeness, happiness, and direction for the day. If my depression, anxiety, anger, and obsessive-compulsive disorder are intense that day, meditation always calms me, even if that calmness is only temporary.

Along with meditation, I tap into my spirituality when I commune with nature. As a mental health speaker, I'm almost constantly traveling. I don't always get a chance to get out of the hotel and enjoy the beautiful time in nature. However, even when I'm traveling, I always make a point to take time and walk outside to get fresh air and enjoy whatever sights and sounds are available.

There's something about the connection to nature that is very, very profound for me. As I continue to grow in my recovery, I further explore my spirituality and what it means to me.

Mental exercise is just as important in my life as physical exercise, and I try to keep my mind working at all times. My goal is to get two hours of reading in each and every day.

I find that when I put in lots of time reading each day, I end up making better decisions. Reading for me isn't just about learning information, it's also about letting information simmer in the back of my mind that will ultimately come through and help me make better decisions later on.

I keep a running list of books I want to read that includes books about mental health, business, and leadership. I learned from several mental health professionals that you can learn a lot about your mental health from reading books on business and leadership.

As I began to read more and more business books, I started to develop better skills to communicate with people, lead teams, and grow my business. I also started to get a deeper understanding of my own mind and how it works.

When it comes to the **physical** side of life, I have been fortunate to have a trainer and nutritionist as a guide in my life. Maik Wiedenbach has been an incredible friend and one of the best resources for transforming stigma into strength for myself.

Since I began working with Maik, I now make it a point to exercise six days a week. I do my best to get to the gym regularly and work in both strength training and cardio to my regular routine.

In addition to exercise, I've also made it a point to watch my nutritional habits. I eat healthier and am intentional about what I eat and why. I enjoy my fair share of junk food, but I am always aware of what I'm putting into my body.

In my journey towards eating healthy, I eat more organically grown food and smaller portions. I also supplement my diet with vitamins and other nutrition supplements. Since I've started intentionally eating healthier, I've had more energy throughout the day.

While many consider their food intake, they after overlook water. Many times when I was convinced I was depressed, sad, stressed, anxious, or angry, I was actually simply dehydrated. Although I believe that my mental health challenges are much more than dehydration, I know to check the amount of water I have been drinking that day as those feelings start to come up.

When I'm starting to feel unstable, I drink two glasses of water, and it often helps me feel a sense of calm. It's also good for your body to drink plenty of water each day. Plus the extra trips to the bathroom will force you to get a little additional exercise.

When people start implementing self-care, they often remember to focus on spiritual, mental, and physical aspects, but they forget **social-emotional.** Mental health challenges and people issues go hand-in-hand. Whether the person is real or imagined, alive or dead, generally, if you have a mental health challenge there is usually at least one person involved. So you need to ensure you have healthy social-emotional interactions.

In order to get myself to a healthier place mentally, I had to take a brutally honest inventory of the people in my life and assess who was bringing in negative energy and who was bringing in positive energy.

Once I was brutally honest with myself, I knew that I had some tough decisions to make. I worked up the courage to distance myself from certain people, whom I loved, and still love, but who were just bringing too much negative energy into my life to justify keeping them close.

To offset the loss of overall relationships in my life, I started to seek out more positive relationships with people (I will cover this in more detail in chapter 11). I have learned when it comes to relationships, you have to be intentional about them. In fact, when it comes to self-care, you have to be intentional about every aspect of it.

This realization inspired me to become more proactive about making plans with friends, colleagues, and people in my social networks each week. On any given week, it's a normal appointment for me to have coffee with someone in New York City. When I travel, I always make it a point to enjoy meals with people that I want to spend time with.

Tim Ferris, author of *The 4-Hour Workweek*, said it best when he stated that the key to happiness is to spend three hours each week with food at a table surrounded by the people that you love. Whenever possible, make it a point to have meals with people you care about, who care about you, and who bring positive and not negative energy into your life.

As I said in the last chapter, we are tribal people by nature. In addition to surrounding myself with positive individuals, I also look for groups of people to connect with. One of the most important groups in my life is my mastermind group.

A mastermind group is a group of people that you can meet with on a regular basis. They serve as your accountability partners; give you advice; feedback and support; and when needed, help you out of difficult situations.

Finally, one of the most important ways I practice self-care is by going to therapy. Therapy does help; you just have to stick with it. Many often feel frustrated because they are looking for quick solutions. Our society is constantly looking for quick solutions to life's challenges, but life's challenges are conquered over time with hard work and determination.

Through attending therapy I have learned an important lesson: life is a never-ending onion with many, many layers. Each time I go to therapy, I peel away a different layer and learn more about myself.

As I discover more, I've become more aware of myself. As I become more aware of myself, I'm better able to deal with my toxic thoughts and feelings. I'm grateful because I believe that working with my therapist consistently for the past several years has helped me avoid several potentially damaging mental health crises.

Taking care of yourself is leadership. If you aren't able to positively impact and lead yourself, it will be hard to positively impact and lead others. Leadership starts internally, and the better you take care of yourself, the better you can care for and help others, especially as a mental wellness superhero.

While I'm not a mental health professional, I've taken responsibility for my recovery and have found what works for me. Taking care of myself includes a wide variety of daily activities and concentrated efforts.

Now it's your turn. Your mission is to take a step towards taking better care of yourself in the next 24 hours. Take a few minutes to answer the following questions:

1. What steps can you take to make sure that you are taking your prescribed medications at the recommended times each day?

2. What are the top three things that you need start doing to improve your overall health?

3. What self-care activity could you begin doing tomorrow for 15 minutes?

4. What do you need to do to start waking up 15 minutes earlier each day to start a morning routine?

5. What steps can you take to make sure that you are getting to your therapy sessions and support group meetings? If you aren't seeing a therapist and attending a support group, please visit the resources page on TransformingStigma.com.

6. Who are the positive people in your life and how can you find ways to spend more quality time with them?

7. What impact do you feel your new self-care habits will have on people you know who are struggling with mental health challenges?

After you answer these questions, plan your next week to work on taking better care of yourself.

You're now well on your way to becoming a superhero. Just remember that every superhero has growing pains as they learn to hone their special set of skills.

While self-care is critical to transforming shame, it's only the beginning. Once you begin to practice it, you will lay a foundation to embrace the confusion that mental health challenges bring.

I encourage you to:

· **Embrace the idea that mental health challenges are con-**

fusing. They aren't always going to make sense. There's not just one way to handle them.

- **Embrace your vulnerability.** It's okay to feel overwhelmed, scared, and out-of-control at times.

- **Embrace the reality that recovery is a process, not a destination.** Get excited about your journey toward self-discovery.

You will have rough weeks, and the makeup of what you need to take care of yourself will change, but by taking an intentional approach to taking care of yourself, you are pledging to embrace your superhero powers. You will improve yourself, those around you, and the world for the better.

Shame leads to silence. However, once you begin practicing self-care, you will feel better about yourself. When you feel better about yourself, it is much easier to talk about mental health challenges.

One of the most important roles of a mental wellness superhero is being a catalyst for conversations. These conversations are often uncomfortable, but so critical to Transforming Stigma™.

CHAPTER 10

TRANSFORMING SILENCE

After having a mental health breakdown in 2011, I decided I would no longer hide my history, hoping no one would ever find out about my mental health challenges. I was starting to feel good about who I was as a person, and I wanted to have authentic relationships with people, which meant being true to myself and not hiding from my current mental health challenges or my history with them.

Just for the record, I can't stand the term "mental illness," hence my use of the term "mental health challenges" in this book It makes me angry, and I feel bad about my struggles. Despite those feelings, I am a troublemaker who likes to stir the pot and get reactions out of people.

My troublemaking self began an experiment that year. Whenever I had the opportunity to introduce myself to someone new, I would introduce myself by saying "Hi, I'm Mike Veny, and I'm mentally ill." The goal was to see what reactions I would get from people in response.

Would people run from me? Would I be shunned? Would I scare or weird people out to the point they would never want to talk to me again?

So what do you think happened?

Surprisingly, not a single person responded to my introduction negatively. That doesn't mean it was always met with joy or some deep connection based on shared struggles with mental health challenges because it wasn't.

Sometimes it was met with frustration or confusion. "I'm mentally ill too... why are we talking about this?" I'd hear. The majority of people, however, responded with curiosity. In fact, during that year, I made more friends, got invited to more parties, and was hit on by more women than I ever have in my entire life.

It became clear that this little experiment was the catalyst for conversations about mental health. This experiment showed me that talking about mental health was beneficial outside of just raising awareness.

It's a conversation that connects us with each other. We're scared to talk about mental health challenges because of the stigma surrounding it. However, the more we avoid talking about it, the longer, and possibly the stronger, stigma will survive.

I learned that discussing mental health could bring people together. How could that be? This was the opposite of what I was taught growing up. From an early age, my parents made it very clear to me that no one could ever find out about my mental health history because it would be tough to get a job; have a romantic relationship; and have a shot at a normal, healthy life. They were trying to protect me but shielding someone from their problems not only hurts that person, it also hurts the communities that could learn and ultimately benefit from this shared knowledge.

The key to transforming the silence around the subject of mental health is simple: **TALK ABOUT IT!** We need to constantly have conversations. Many of us suffer in silence but we thrive when we communicate and work together on solutions.

Because I was willing to open up and discuss what used to be a scary topic , I made friends, found a therapist, found my future wife, learned more about myself, and learned how to overcome the challenges I faced and still face today. When you decide to openly talk about your mental health challenges, you take power away from those challenges.

When something is bottled up inside of you, and you feel that you have to hide it from the world, it owns you. It controls you.

Since the only way to overcome it is to take control back, you have to let it out, and that happens with conversation.

Think about your boobies for a second. That's right; I said your boobies. Before you get offended or think that I'm just being crass, I'd like to introduce you to the Feel Your Boobies® Foundation. Breast cancer was a taboo topic several decades ago. Through working diligently to keep the subject in conversation, organizations like the Feel Your Boobies® Foundation have empowered women to get tested and have raised money to help find a cure.

According to their website, *"The Feel Your Boobies® Foundation is a breast cancer non-profit that promotes proactive breast health in young women."* Feel Your Boobies® is just one of hundreds of breast health awareness and breast cancer awareness organizations around the world. These organizations help raise funding for research and increase our understanding of the deadly disease.

There is no cure for breast cancer, at least not yet. However, the stigma surrounding it has transformed dramatically according to Braun S. "Breast cancer was surrounded by secrecy until the 1980s, when brave individuals such as former First Ladies Betty Ford and Nancy Reagan; and founder of the Susan G. Komen Foundation, Nancy Brinker (Susan Komen's sister), began speaking publicly about the personal impact of the disease, which increased awareness of breast cancer and made it more acceptable to talk about it openly." [20]

If not for their efforts, it's very likely that the secrecy and lack of conversation surrounding breast cancer would have continued, and may still exist today, just as it does around mental health.

In the same way the brave women who battled both breast cancer and the stigma surrounding it helped raise awareness and millions of dollars, I have decided that full disclosure is the only choice if I am truly committed to Transforming Stigma™.

If I want to help foster change, I can't pick and choose what to share or hold back because it may be slightly uncomfortable. Change is uncomfortable for a reason—something is changing. While I can't say that you absolutely should or shouldn't disclose your mental health state or history, there are four reasons you should consider having conversations about it:

---

20   S. Braun. "The history of breast cancer advocacy." The breast journal. Accessed December 2017. https://www.ncbi.nlm.nih.gov/pubmed/12713506.

1. It takes the elephant out of the room.

If you are struggling with a mental health challenges, chances are that someone in your life is aware of it. If someone has detected it, they may not address it with you out of fear of your reaction or simply because it is an uncomfortable subject but they may address their suspicions with others.

While you may see this as someone talking behind your back, it isn't always malicious or intended to turn people against you. We all want confirmation that an observation we've made is true or not. Discussing with our peer groups is how we validate these observations and beliefs.

When you take the initiative and discuss your challenges openly and honestly, it clears the air and makes this uncomfortable subject a bit more comfortable to talk about. You also prevent future untrue rumors by setting the record straight immediately and opening a line of communication where you and others can both learn more about and discuss mental health challenges.

For example, if you and I became friends, I may worry about losing you as a friend if you were to find out about my mental health challenges. On days where I am feeling depressed, anxious, angry, or obsessing, I may worry that you are going to talk about me behind my back, judge me, and/or choose not be my friend because I am different.

I had this concern in the back of my mind in the past partly because my parents discouraged me from discussing it.

They weren't trying to make life more difficult for me; they cared about me and wanted the best for me. However, they truly believed that keeping this information locked inside and away from the world was in my best interest.

If you and I do become friends (you never know), I would now let you know about my challenges not to elicit sympathy or attention but in order to help you understand some of my behavior.

Honesty and information are both important in relationships. Addressing and talking about problems with those around you establishes trust and opens the line of communication about an otherwise difficult topic.

2. It makes you feel less burdened.

Living in New York City, I use public transportation to get around. On busy days, when I have appointments throughout the city, I take along my backpack, which I wear throughout the entire day. I do my best to pack as light as possible and stick with the essentials (laptop, chargers, water, food, etc.), but it still weighs 10-20 pounds.

By the end of the day, my back aches as I walk home. Once I get in the door, I take off my backpack and feel the burdens of the day hit the floor along with it. At that moment, I feel lighter and free.

Trying to keep that secret on your back all day and letting it control the way you think, communicate, and interact with the people in your life puts significant weight on your shoulders, taking a toll on your mind and your life. Staying silent about your mental health challenges is like having a heavy backpack on your shoulders 24/7.

When I decided to share this with people, each time, I took the weight off of my shoulders. Once you begin discussing them with people in your life, you will immediately feel lighter and free.

3. It helps you get the help you need

When I was younger, I had a fear of elevators. If I hadn't faced that fear and instead taken the stairs every time I needed to go up or down in a building, I never would have entered that scary, little, old elevator where I met my therapist (true story).

An elevator ride can still trigger my anxiety, but completely avoiding them denies me the opportunity to face one of my fears and address the problem, which can help provide some of the help I need to get well.

As our society moves closer to Transforming Stigma™, people are becoming more educated about the subject of mental health and available resources. When you openly disclose, you never know who may be able to provide you with the help that you need.

4. You can help others through those conversations

Recently, I had a meltdown in front of a family member. He told me he cared about me and just wanted me to get help. After that, he never asked about my mental health or how I was doing. I fear this is how too many of us view someone struggling with a mental health challenges. They just need to simply get help or get it out of their system, and that's it—they're cured.

While getting help is critical to recovery, it's almost equally important to keep it in everyday conversation and to constantly and consistently work to minimize any negative effects of mental health challenges. I tell everybody that I go to therapy. I tell them when I've had a breakthrough or a challenging session. I tell them when I've felt depressed or have had a panic attack.

The more I share, the more they understand, and not just about me but about themselves. As I've encouraged people to make this subject a part of normal everyday conversations, I have seen miracles.

"Personal disclosure of narrative accounts is an essential tool for change, given its potential to humanize mental illness." [21]

One of my friends was having a difficult time with his job. His boss was stressing him out and acting very strangely. When he first told me about it, he was frustrated because of his boss's "mental disease" and didn't know what to do about it.

The moment the words "mental disease" came out of his mouth, I got angry. And I mean really angry. That phrase is a product of the stigma surrounding mental health. Despite my frustration, I listened with an open heart and gave him words of support and encouragement to get through his difficult time.

As time went on, I made it a point to regularly discuss my mental health challenges with him. My friend did the best that he could to listen to me and gain a greater understanding of mental health challenges. He soon began to speak about his boss with more compassion, despite his boss still behaving in a manner that confused him. He developed compassion because we began to make mental health part of our normal conversations.

Another time, a man approached me after a speech at a youth mental health conference in California. He told me that he was a mental health professional and found my speech inspiring, but he was hesitant with one aspect of my talk: making mental health a part of everyday conversation.

He felt that his colleagues would judge him. In fact, he told me

---

21   Stephen P. Henshaw. The mark of shame: stigma of mental illness and an agenda for change. New York, NY: Oxford University Press, 2010.

that he was advised to never speak about his own mental health challenges in the workplace.

"How ironic." I said to him. "Mental health professionals are in the business of serving people with mental health challenges, yet they can't talk about their own challenges. Do you find that strange?" He took a second to think about it. "Yes," he said defensively, "but that's the culture in my workplace. You just don't talk about your "challenges."

He isn't alone. Millions of people across the country fear discussing their challenges, even in places that should be safe.

"Sir, may I challenge you to a bet?" I asked. "Ummmm... depends on what the bet is," which is a good answer when anyone challenges you to a bet. "I bet you that if you start to open up about your own mental health challenges, you will develop a deeper connection with the clients you serve and your colleagues."

He had a look of fear in his eyes. I assumed that he wouldn't do it, and I understood his concerns as I once was afraid to share my mental health struggles with anyone. Regardless, I kept going. "If I am right, then you can take me out to dinner at the best steak place that you know of the next time I come to California." He looked at me with a half smile, shook my hand, and said, "deal."

I was confident that I would never hear from him again, but the opportunity was far greater than the risk in my opinion. If he did take me up on my bet, it would mean that he would open up to his colleagues and his clients and start important conversations that included his struggles instead of only discussing the mental health challenges of others. While this can feel like a tremendous risk for the person sharing their challenges, I have yet to have challenged someone to share their struggles with others and heard back from them that they regret doing it.

Several months later, I received this email:

SUBJECT: Steak

BODY:

Mike,

I don't know if you remember me. My name is John Johnson. You and I spoke after your presentation in California. You suggested that I be more open in my workplace about my mental health challenges.

I decided to take you up on your bet and couldn't believe the response. Some of my most difficult clients are making more progress, and many of my colleagues have been coming to me to discuss their mental health challenges.

I really appreciate you talking with me and will gladly buy you a steak dinner the next time you are in California.

John Johnson

I have yet to enjoy my free steak dinner, but I'm excited to hear more about how he has opened up to his clients and colleagues, and how that has continued to impact his work.

Let's be clear: talking about your mental health, or that of a loved one, doesn't mean you have to discuss every little detail. For example, when people talk about their cancer treatment, they don't usually talk about changes in sexual function, which for some cancer treatments is a side effect.

I am not suggesting that you share personal information and details with others if you're not comfortable with it. However, I am encouraging you to find ways to begin opening up about it.

Talking about it is a start.

Much of the perceived negativity that inhibits people from having these conversations comes from ignorance. People are ignorant because they lack information, understanding, and awareness.

They aren't used to talking about it. And they can't accurately see these challenges from someone else's point of view if they aren't familiar with that point of view. This is why it's so important to keep the subject of mental health in our everyday conversations.

"The media are a large, some believe the principal, source of stigma."[22] However, I believe that it's ultimately a good thing that the media is talking about it even if the majority of that coverage is negative or inaccurate—at least it's in the conversation.

As a musician and speaker, I have been fortunate enough to have corporate sponsors. One day, one of my sponsors called a meeting to bring several influencers together.

The focus of the meeting was to discuss strategies about expanding the brand into the health and wellness industry. We were asked to introduce ourselves.

We all knew each other, so it just felt like a formality. As we went around the room, each influencer detailed their unique career path and explained why they were passionate about their work. Then it was my turn.

"My name is Mike Veny. I am mentally ill, and I work with people from all over the country who have challenges like me. I know that everyone has pain, but I don't believe that anyone should have to suffer."

There was silence. Painful, awkward silence. Ten seconds later,

22   Patrick W. Corrigan., David Roe, and Hector W. H. Stang. Challenging the stigma of mental illness: lessons for therapists and advocates. Chichester, West Sussex, UK: John Wiley & Sons, 2011

the meeting moved on as if I had just given a normal introduction like the others.

At the end of our meeting, one of the other influencers came up to me and asked if we could talk. Looking over his shoulder, I saw two others also waiting to talk with me.

It was the same conversation with each person. They thanked me for sharing my mental health struggles. They also shared stories of their mental health challenges and the stories of others. .

I was encouraged by their interest in discussing with me how they resonated with what I had to say. But what I found most interesting was that despite people appreciating me bringing up the subject and coming up to me to talk, they still discussed it as though it were something they should keep secret. They waited until they felt safe to discuss it with me, since I had already shared, instead of bringing it up to discuss with the entire group.

Conversation is a superpower in the fight to transform the stigma surrounding mental health. Like any superpower, it takes a dedicated superhero to get the most out of that superpower and use it properly. To utilize the superpower of conversation, follow the seven C's of having conversations around mental health:

1. Calmness

Discussing mental health can trigger a variety of emotions. Remain calm when discussing the subject. This will ensure you are contributing to a conversation rather than a potentially harmful argument, although I believe there can be benefits gained from both.

To practice remaining calm, rehearse conversations out loud with yourself. This simple technique will help you feel more prepared for real conversations and help anticipate what others might say and how they may react. While I don't recommend putting so much pressure on yourself that you're anxious and nervous about having these conversations, they are important, and the more care and time you put into them, including preparing for them, the more likely they will go well. .

2. Control

One of the lessons many of us learned as children was to "think before you speak." It's a lesson that we can apply to mental health discussions. As you begin rehearsing conversations with yourself, you will get a better sense of what is okay to say and what would be best to leave out.

For example, I say to people that "I was diagnosed with psychosexual disorder as a teenager." If I didn't use control, I would say to people that "As a teenager, I made it a point to try to have sex with any woman that would let me." What you say will have a significant impact on the conversation and how the other person or people view what you're saying.

Showing control in how you speak will keep the conversation on track and maintain the potential impact of your words. You do not have to code or hide details to take out the shock of what you have to share, but you may want to consider how it will come across and if it will further the conversation or take it a step back—this is why control is important.

3. Consistency

As you learn to speak calmly about mental health and control what you say, it's important to focus on being consistent with what you say. As I said earlier, I don't like the terms "mental illness" (despite the fact that my TEDx talk is titled "Mental Illness is an Asset").

I do my best to remember to let people know that I "live with mental health challenges." Keeping it consistent makes it easier for others to respond to you and develop their personal thoughts and beliefs on a subject.

Think of consistency as the motto of a burger franchise. If you see ten commercials for this franchise that all say "You're going to love our buns," that message is going to stick with you. If each commercial shares something different, it will be hard to keep each message straight and to remember every ad.

4. Compassion

You never know what someone else is struggling with. Keep that in mind as you get more comfortable discussing the subject of mental health. It's important to feel and show compassion for anyone you're talking to.

Simply being aware that this may be a sensitive subject will go a long way in making others feel comfortable. And without showing compassion, the person or people you're speaking to are more likely to feel that you are attacking or judging them, which can become a barrier that gets in the way of having a meaningful conversation.

5. Confidence

As a professional speaker, in addition to being knowledgeable and passionate, the power of my message relies on presenting myself in a certain way. If I were presenting on a stage in front of you and mumbled under my breath, looked nervous, and constantly asked for reassurance, it really wouldn't matter how powerful my words were. You would feed off of my lack of confidence and start to feel unsure about me as well.

You must be confident in the way you approach conversations, especially around the subject of mental health. You don't need to be an industry-leading expert on the topic, but you have to be confident enough to talk about it and to be there for others to share what they want to share and discuss the topic with them.

6. Context

Have you ever came into the middle of a joke and not had a clue what everyone was laughing about? Trying to jump into a conversation about mental health challenges you or someone else may be suffering from isn't nearly as effective as providing some sort of context or finding the right time or opportunity to talk about it.

7. Clarity

Mental health, and what it means, is surrounded by confusion. To better guide and have discussions on the topic, you should have a clear understanding of what particular terms mean to you, and why. If you're not clear what it means to you, the conversations you have and the people you speak with may end up being more confused after your discussion than before it.

Practice having clarity by investing the time in researching different terms that you wish to discuss. These definitions may take a different shape and form after having discussions, but by having clear ideas of what each means to you, the conversations you have will clarify what you think about them.

People-First Language

While saying "Hi, I'm Mike Veny and I'm mentally ill" was a doorway to many conversations for me, I don't suggest using that language when having conversations. In my ignorance, I was giving myself a label. What I've learned since then is that it's important to not make someone's health challenges their identity.

"In Batman: The Dark Knight, Batman describes one of the Joker's henchman as a paranoid schizophrenic, 'the type of mind attracted to the villian.' Three years earlier was Batman begins. A corrupted psychiatrist had planned to put a drug in the water supply which caused people to have psychotic episodes....

Many advocates support person-first language to challenge stigma. In this view, people are referred to as a 'person' plus the condition: a person with mental illness, people with schizophrenia, people taking medication. This language reminds us that individuals with mental illness are people first; namely their character and assets centrally reside in their identity as a person." [23]

Here are some examples of how to use people-first language:

Don't say: "mentally ill people"

Do say: "people living with mental health challenges"

Don't say: "He's bipolar"

Do say: "He's a person living with bipolar disorder"

Don't say: "She's autistic"

Do say: "She has autism"

For more examples, please visit the resources page on TransformingStigma.com.

Finally, it's important to be aware of the overall language we use everyday.

Take for instance, someone saying, "She's a little more than strange - she's psycho." [24] What often seems like an innocent description of a person can hurt someone for a lifetime.

Keeping mental health in our everyday conversations has the

---

23   Corrigan, Roe, Stang, Challenging the Stigma
24   Henshaw, The Mark of Shame

power to change lives and laws, increase support and mental health programing and funding, and decrease the stigma surrounding mental health. So take a deep breath, think about your boobies, and start talking about it (not your boobies, mental health)!

Even though most of us know that other people experience mental health challenges or know people who do, we often feel alone in our journey. This is why silence leads to sabotage, self-destructive behavior, social injustice, and suicide. In this chapter, you'll learn how to transform this through connecting with other people.

Conversation is the beginning of connecting. As you begin to have better conversations using "people-first" language, be aware of the tendency to constantly correct others who are using stigmatizing language. When you focus on correcting, you aren't connecting.

CHAPTER 11

TRANSFORMING SABOTAGE, SOCIAL INJUSTICE, SELF DESTRUCTIVE BEHAVIOR, & SUICIDE

As a child sitting on the floor of my mother's bedroom watching television, I felt connected to the characters I watched day after day. However, Big Bird and Ernie on Sesame Street didn't feel the same way because they couldn't connect with me.

Despite their inability to connect with me individually, I looked up to, learned from, and trusted them—I felt connected. And we all need and crave connections.

John Kim, Licensed Marriage and Family Therapist, explained in a Psychology Today blog post, "We are born connected. We feel whole. The second our umbilical cord is cut, we feel alone. Incomplete. From here on out, we crave connection."[25]

So what is a connection? The type of connection we're discussing in this chapter is defined by Merriam-Webster as "a person connected with another especially by marriage, kinship, or common interest."[26] Connections are strong and should always be beneficial for both parties.

One-sided relationships, like my admiration for a tall feathered puppet or a rabid fan of a punk rock band, have meaning for those who have developed the feeling of an actual connection. But this is not a true connection, and we're still left craving real connections when our lives only consist of one-sided relationships.

In the movie *Cast Away*, Tom Hanks plays Chuck Noland, a man who is the lone survivor of a horrific plane crash. Without anyone to connect with on a deserted island, Hank befriends a Wilson volleyball. He talks to and takes care of the volleyball like he is his best friend, but Wilson couldn't satisfy his natural need for healthy, mutually-beneficial, two-way connections.

On a deeper scale, we have our pets. We love our pets, and they play an important role in our lives. I've struggled to recover from the loss of my last two pets.

---

25   John Kim. "Why We Need More Connection." July 26, 2017. Accessed December 2017. https://www.psychologytoday.com/blog/the-angry-therapist/201707/why-we-need-more-connection.

26   Merriam-Webster, s.v. "connection," accessed December 2017. https://www.merriam-webster.com/dictionary/connection

People laugh and think I'm joking when I tell them that I cried when my hamster died, and it took several years before I was ready to purchase another pet—a betta fish, who recently died while I was traveling. While pets can connect with us on some level, more so than a fictional character and an inanimate object, they don't completely satisfy our need for connections, Regardless whether or not either of my pets felt a connection with me, they brought joy into my life, and I was genuinely upset when they left.

These one-sided relationships, whether with a volleyball or betta fish, can help us get through tough times, but they are not a replacement for real, deep human connections. I've ditched my television and now focus on seeking out the relationships I need—strong connections with other humans like Cheryl Williams who convinced me to speak at her event, and Michael Luchies, a friend who also has mental health challenges and worked with me on this book.

Both are people I could call day or night about problems in my business, relationships, or mental health and trust that they are genuinely trying to help. At the darkest times in my life, it has been these types of connections that have saved my life and helped me recover when I was ready to give up.

As a professional speaker and musician, I meet and speak with tens of thousands of people each year. Most of my deep connections have not developed from these encounters; they have come from intentionally seeking out help and support, and through working hard to develop and maintain the relationship.

On the other hand, some of my deepest connections and most beneficial relationships have come from support groups and twelve-step programs. There are support groups for nearly anyone, including those who live with or are interested in learning more about their own mental health.

Organizations including Emotions Anonymous, the Depression and Bipolar Support Alliance, NAMI, and support groups hosted by Mental Health America give people a way and a reason to connect with others dealing with similar challenges through support groups. Groups like these have changed my life for the better, and I highly recommend that you consider participating in a session with an open mind. These are places where I can be myself, where I can be my broken self with all of my flaws, and share about my challenges without being judged or condemned for what I'm thinking, my actions, or for disclosing my challenges with my own mental health.

Conversations, like a discussion with members of a support group, lead to connections. And connections lead to deep and meaningful relationships that can change the world. A single powerful conversation is akin to Batman stopping a robbery.

A connection, however, brings superheroes together for a greater cause than just a single event. Instead of Batman stopping a robbery (a conversation), a connection is Batman and Robin teaming together to foil The Joker's plot to destroy Gotham City, or Marvel's The Avengers teaming up together to save the world from evil.

What's a protest with one person? How powerful is a nonprofit with one employee? A connection is a movement compared to a conversation, which is like a single idea—powerful but in need of support to grow into more. And support, which comes with connection, is what we all need.

People who can rally others to support themselves or a cause can change the world. Say what you will about political figures like Barack Obama or Donald Trump but they have found ways to generate support and create connections that have led to them making changes that they believe are best for the world.

We often fail to make those deep, meaningful connections with others, which contributes to us being less aware of the people in our lives. When watching a television interview with a family member, friend, or neighbor of someone accused of committing a crime or taking their own life, what's the first comment we frequently hear that person make? "I never saw any warning signs," or "I didn't think they were capable of this."

How could we be so bad at recognizing warning signs exhibited by the people that are so close to us?.

First, we didn't develop a deep enough relationship with them. Because of this, we're not looking for or able to recognize these warning signs. Second, as a society, our social skills are in serious need of help, and we're not nearly as good at communicating with others as we think.

We need to focus on developing real, deep connections. Since mental health is comprised of my thoughts, feelings, and behaviors, and my thoughts are influenced by relationships, the stronger my relationships are, the healthier my thoughts are. Addictions, for example, aren't just about the substance that's being abused. My relationships and connections play a significant role in my mental health challenges.

When I form deep connections, I feel empowered to rise above my mental health challenges and help others. The more I'm able to bring people into my life, the more I'm able to help others break down and transform the stigma surrounding mental health.

Like anything worth building, a connection takes time, and it doesn't come without a conversation. Spending years nurturing connections to transform stigma, I've found that for me, seven components are necessary to create meaningful connections.

While not every step is required each time, think of these as ingredients to a wonderful meal—the more you add, the better it becomes. But if you over or under-season the food, it might not come out right, so adjust your recipe as needed. The ingredients of a strong connection include: taking inventory of your relationships, consistently educating yourself, learning the signs and symptoms of someone who is struggling, sharing your story, supporting someone who is struggling, and becoming a fierce advocate.

Take Inventory of Your Relationships

As I mentioned in Chapter 9 (Transforming Shame), mental health challenges and people issues go hand-in-hand. You can't have one without the other.

I want this book to *move* you to action. But before you can move, you need to decide who is staying behind and who is coming along with you.

I want you to take inventory of the relationships in your life, and decide which ones are worth building, which ones are already strong connections that you can continue to nurture, and which relationships are better to distance yourself from. You don't have to cut people out of your life, but taking inventory can help you determine whom you should spend more time around, and whom to love from afar.

When I decided to take inventory of the people in my life, I wrote down every person I knew, and next to their name, I wrote how I felt before interacting with them, in their presence, and after interacting with them. For example, when it came to interacting with my mother, whom I love dearly, I often felt anxious when I knew I was going to see her, frustrated when in her presence, and depressed after interacting with her.

Although I love and she is my mother, I made the decision to minimize my contact with her so I could have the time, energy, and mental capacity to expand on the positive connections in my life. This doesn't mean I cut my mother out of my life, I simply gained a better understanding of her impact on me and my life, and made a decision on how I would approach spending, or not spending, time on the relationship in the near future.

This was both a painful and exciting experience. It was like weighing myself for the first time in a year when I knew I had lost a lot of weight.

I had to face where I was at, and then decide how best to move forward. So while I had to make significant changes in the people I spent time and energy on, I also recognized opportunities to grow connections that could have a significant positive impact on myself and others.

When creating this list and analyzing each relationship, do your best to not label people in your life as good or bad. Just be brutally honest with yourself about who brings you joy and who doesn't. I've been lucky to have many amazingly caring, talented, and generous people in my life whom I have just not connected with for one reason or another.

The timing might not be right or our personalities clash, but there is nothing wrong or bad with this person, nor are they forever banned from my life. I just choose to love some people in my life from afar, but I don't need to talk to them each day, month, year, or even decade.

As you take inventory of the people in your life, you may have to muster the courage to put close family members on the list of people you can live without, as I did. As you can imagine, it's not that easy, and with every toxic relationship in your life, you may share some of the blame for why it turned sour.

To foster healthy relationships, you want to make sure you create boundaries. According to the book, *Boundaries: When to Say Yes, How to Say No To Take Control of Your Life by Dr. Henry Cloud,* which I highly recommend reading, "A boundary is a personal property line that marks those things for which we are responsible. In other words, boundaries define who we are and who we are not."[27]

Earlier in my life, I failed to create boundaries, open up conversations about what was and wasn't acceptable, and what my needs were with people. If people don't know what you want and what you are and aren't okay with, it's hard for them to ever properly approach their relationship with you in a way that is going to help both you and them. And the longer you go without setting boundaries, the more damage is done to the relationship, and the more damage you incur because of your failure to set boundaries.

Imagine you have just begun a new romantic relationship, or at least you hope it will turn into a romantic relationship. It's your first date, and you've decided to take your date out to dinner.

Trying to make a good impression, you say, "I'd like to take you anywhere you'd like to go." They reply, "How about Benny's Pizza?" You pause for a second, realizing your date has no idea that you once got food poisoning from Benny's Pizza and haven't eaten a slice of pizza in three years, and say, "Sounds great!"

Five years later, you're married, and your sweetheart asks why you haven't finished the Benny's leftovers in the fridge, and you explode in a fit of rage explaining you hate Benny's Pizza. It's not their

27   Henry Cloud. Boundaries: When to Say Yes, How to Say No to Take Control of Your Life. Harpercollins Christian Pub, 2017.

fault you never took the effort to set boundaries and speak your mind to them.

When taking an honest look at your relationships and how you should move them forward or scale them back, consider the boundaries you have or haven't set that are getting in the way of building healthy, meaningful connections with the people in your life. And for all of the relationships in your life, set boundaries.

You owe it to yourself and to them to explain what you're comfortable with and what needs to stop. If they can't respect the boundaries you set, first consider if they are reasonable, and then consider how important these boundaries are in order to maintain your mental health, and growing forward to help others in your life.

Taking inventory is an ongoing process, but the first time you take inventory of your relationships, you'll begin to enjoy more beneficial relationships that will enrich your life, and put aside the relationships that are hurting your growth and potential to have a superhero-like impact on the people you love and the world.

Constantly Educate Yourself

Through learning, we grow as people, which is something we should strive for daily. The crusade to transform stigma likely won't end before the time I pass on from this world, but I will take every opportunity until that day to work on empowering myself and others to change the world by improving the lives of those who live with their own mental health challenges, and the mental health challenges of their loved ones.

It's never too late to learn and never too early to start. Much can be accomplished through hard work, but we limit our growth when we aren't educating ourselves.

"Education programs help identify the myths of mental illness and the facts that challenge these myths."[28] As a mental wellness superhero, educating yourself has three components: Listening, Learning, and Language. Let's explore each.

- **Listening:** Listen in on others conversations about particular topics of meaning for you within the subject of mental health, such as depression, suicide prevention, etc. While I'm not suggesting eavesdropping on private conversations, social media allows you to listen in on public conversations.

- **Learning:** Learn about laws that affect people with mental health challenges, the most up-to-date terminology used to discuss mental health challenges, and the latest trends in treatment.

- **Language:** In chapter 10, I introduced you to "people-first" language. It's important to know the current terminology people use to discuss mental challenges and also understand that it is constantly evolving. Even some of the terminology in this book might be considered politically incorrect by the time you read it.

Most of my education in managing my own mental health challenges and Transforming Stigma™ has come from reading. I apply what I learn in my own life and share it with others, like through this book. For my full list of recommended books and resources, visit the Resources page on TransformingStigma.com.

For every superhero working to fight an evil villain, getting stronger and continued training is an important aspect of their life. Make it a part of yours. Whether you spend five minutes reading each

---

28   Patrick W. Corrigan., David Roe, and Hector W. H. Stang. *Challenging the stigma of mental illness: lessons for therapists and advocates.* Chichester, West Sussex, UK: John Wiley & Sons, 2011.

night before going to bed or read one blog post online about mental health each day, make a commitment to educate yourself—you will rarely regret time spent learning. What you learn has the power to change your life and spread from your mind to others, especially if you follow the steps on how to create strong and mutually beneficial connections.

Learn the Signs and Symptoms of Someone Who is Struggling

I am not a mental health professional. I am simply a man who lives with depression, anxiety, obsessive-compulsive disorder, and seeks to help others. I can't give you an educated and unique breakdown of the long list of signs and symptoms of what to look for in someone who is struggling but there are many resources for you to learn the signs and symptoms of mental health challenges.

The best place to begin learning is the internet. As you learn, memorize the signs and symptoms like the back of your hand. By knowing when someone may be struggling with a mental health challenge you can better understand their needs and how to meet them.

You will never have all of the answer but if you better understand problems, you will be able to work with someone to lead them towards the solutions they need without needing to diagnose them, which you should never do unless you are a mental health professional qualified to do so.

In my opinion, the most important mental health challenge to know the signs and symptoms for is suicide. If you know what to look for there, you can quickly detect if someone in your life is contemplating it.

Take a first step and search for the signs and symptoms of mental health challenges. Go online and search for symptoms. Use this information carefully and keep in mind that any person can exhibit signs of a mental health challenge, and in tough times in their life, they need help and support.

Share Your Story

Facts touch our minds and stories touch our heart. That's why I started this book's introduction with a few facts, and then went right into my story, hoping that it may touch your heart at some level.

After all, we "Bring it home by telling good stories illustrated with concrete experiences."[29]

In the book, Challenging the Stigma of Mental Illness, the authors share some guidelines on how to be effective when sharing story about yourself, a family member, or a friend:

- Be personal. Talk about one's experiences.
  - Write (or speak) from the heart
  - Not too formal
- Be concrete and to the point.
- Use and define professional terms where needed.
- Be truthful.
  - Don't hide the facts
  - Don't over-embellish
- Only discuss those things one is comfortable talking about.
- Keep it short and focused.

29   Corrigan, Roe, Stang, *Challenging the Stigma*

- Provide specific examples of illness where needed.
- No skeletons in the childhood closet.
  - The impact of disease onset
  - Struggling with some failures
  - The impact on family
  - Slowly coming to grips and winning
- Tackle the impact of stigma head on.
  - The effect of others judgements
- Remember the moral of the story.
  - "I work, live, and play, *just like everyone*[30]

I travel the world and share my story with audiences. The toughest part of sharing my story is knowing that so many people have experienced many of the same challenges, some worse, and some have died because of them. However, because of the stigma surrounding mental health, few share their story. I can tell you from experience that your story matters and has the potential to save someone's life.

After I'm finished with a presentation, people often form a line to speak with me because they have felt a connection to my story, become empowered, and want to share with me a detail about their life that they rarely, if ever, share. Simply listening to my story empowered them to seek out a connection with me.

In late 2017, the hashtag #MeToo spread across the world as women shared their stories of sexual harassment. As the movement grew, more and more women came out, and as they shared their stories, changes began to take place.

---

30   Corrigan, Roe, Stang, *Challenging the Stigma*

Well-known movie stars and television personalities who had allegedly been harassing men and women for years were fired, resigned, and even replaced in movies they were previously a part of. Sharing the difficult parts of your life can be scary, but these stories can influence and empower others who have not yet felt able to share their own story.

Start talking. Your story is a superpower!

I recommend starting by sharing small, relevant anecdotes with people in your life. When someone says they are struggling because they are on a new medication, share the time you couldn't sleep because of an antidepressant.

When you hear someone say "What are you crazy?" tell them that you do have challenges with your mental health, and you'd be happy to talk to them about it. When you begin to share, others open up to you, and you start to feel comfortable telling your story.

Support Others Who Are Struggling

"Most people do not listen with the intent to understand; they listen with the intent to reply."

— Stephen R. Covey

As a professional speaker, my career relies on me talking. But when I'm done talking, and anytime I'm not on stage, my job is to listen, and it's a more important job than reciting a speech and even telling my life's story.

Just as there can't be a connection without a conversation, no meaningful conversation can take place without listening. Without listening, a potentially meaningful connection turns into, at best, a one-sided relationship like mine with the characters on Sesame Street. To help someone, we have to know them, and to know them, we need to listen to them.

To listen, ask good questions and remember, after you've asked each question, to shut up. Say, "Help me understand"... and shut up. "How can I support you?"... and shut up. Listen to what they say, how they act, and ask questions. Stay away from making assumptions.

The hardest part about listening is holding back your urge to immediately respond, share, and help. Your goal isn't to solve their problems or explain how everything is going to be okay—it's to listen. Listen with the intent to understand.

Along with listening to others, one of the best ways to support others who are struggling (and help yourself is to become part of advocacy groups) such as:

1. American Foundation for Suicide Prevention (AFSP)

2. National Alliance on Mental Illness (NAMI)

3. Mental Health America (MHA)

4. National Federation of Families for Children's Mental Health (NFFCMH)

5. Depression and Bipolar Support Alliance (DBSA)

These groups have national, state, and local chapters. For an up-to-date list of advocacy organizations, please visit the Resources page on TransformingStigma.com.

Become a Fierce Advocate

Many of the youth who get arrested and tried in New York State (and all over the country) have many unmet mental health needs. It's through the advocacy of family-run organizations, like Families

Together New York State, that more youth and families will have the opportunity to get their mental health needs met, giving them a greater shot at success in life.

Under the leadership of Executive Director Paige Pierce, they worked diligently to raise the age of criminal responsibility to 18 years old in New York State. Prior to this, New York state was one of the few states where people as young as 16 years old were being prosecuted and tried as adults. The goal of the effort was not to give youth a "get out of jail free card" for criminal behavior, but rather to find more effective ways to help them turn their lives around and protect them against the violence from older, incarcerated criminals.

And speaking of crime, one of the most problematic crimes in the United States of America is mass shootings. At the time of this writing, the federal government defines a mass shooting as an event where at least four victims are killed by a firearm. Also at the time of this writing, sadly, the five deadliest mass shootings in US history have occurred in the past 10 years.

In the search for an explanation as to why someone would engage in such a horrific act of violence, conversations come up about the state of someone's mental health as a catalyst for pulling the trigger. Is there a link between mental health challenges and gun violence? Are people with mental health challenges violent and dangerous?

According to the National Alliance on Mental Illness (NAMI), "Having a mental health condition does not make a person more likely to be violent or dangerous. The truth is living with a mental health condition makes you more likely to be a victim of violence, four times the rate of the general public. Studies have shown that 1 in 4 individuals living with a mental health condition will experience some form of violence in any given year."

So what is the link between mental health and violence? The answer to this varies depending on who you ask. Maybe the answer is there is a link in some cases and not others.

The American Psychological Association is taking a proactive approach to this. According to their website, they are advocating for "a public health approach to gun violence prevention, supporting evidence-based programs and policies that can reduce the occurrence and impact of firearm-related violence in the United States."[31]

This includes enhancing access to mental health services and funding research projects looking into the cause of violence. Does this mean they acknowledge mental health could play a role in violence? I am not sure.

If it does play a role, one of the proposed solutions is to create legislation that prevents people with a mental health diagnosis from purchasing firearms. If I was a gun owner who believes in his rights under the Second Amendment of the United States Constitution (the right of the people to keep and bear Arms), then why would I want to seek mental health treatment knowing they would take away my firearm if I did so?

The answers are unclear to me, but it's the start of a conversation. Conversation leads to connection. Families Together New York State, the National Alliance on Mental Illness, and the American Psychological Association are connecting to people through advocacy, along with many other organizations.

Merriam Webster's Dictionary defines advocacy as "the act or

---

31 American Psychological Association. Accessed December 2017. http://www.apa.org/.

process of supporting a cause or proposal."[32] One of the biggest challenges you will undertake as a mental wellness superhero is to become an fierce advocate for mental health.

Your advocacy can include speaking, writing, advertising to create awareness, protests against injustices, petitions to change laws, or fundraising for an organization. Regardless of how you choose to advocate, you will come up against your biggest villain in the process: HATERS. A hater is someone who is negative, critical, or dislikes whatever it is that you are advocating for.

Here are two ways that I've found effective in dealing with haters:

6. If you encounter an individual hater, be intentional about nurturing the relationship and look for every teachable moment to introduce them to a proactive mental health conversation. Although focused on customer service, a great book to check out is *Hug Your Haters* by Jay Baer. The lessons can be easily applied to mental health advocacy.

7. If you encounter a group of haters, run to the conflict and protest.

Regardless of how you go about connecting, it's important that you are consistent.

Building relationships is a learned skill. Sure, for some people, aspects of relationship building may come naturally, but being good at it comes with practice. Have you ever been to an event with someone who seems to know everyone?

This doesn't happen without having strong social skills. And that person, because of their ability and willingness to have conversations and make connections, now has an audience they're connect-

---

32   Merriam-Webster, s.v. "advocacy," accessed December 2017. https://www.merriam-webster.com/dictionary/advocacy

ed with, and with that audience comes the power to positively impact hundreds, and even thousands of lives.

In Stephen Covey's *The Seven Habits of Highly Effective People*, Covey introduces a metaphor where he compares relationships to bank accounts. He calls them Emotional Bank Accounts. In relationships, you can make deposits and withdrawals.

As you make consistent deposits into the Emotional Bank Account of a specific relationship, your relationship grows stronger and you earn trust with the others in this relationship. Each time you break someone's trust in a relationship, you make a withdrawal. If you make too many withdrawals, or one costly one, your account will go negative, and may even need to be closed.[33]

Build relationships by making deposits. Invest in relationships by building trust, giving freely, listening, and finding ways to add value to the lives of others.

Just as every 3,000 miles, you should change your oil, you should also make the time to make emotional deposits. Can you go over 3,000 miles without changing your oil? Absolutely, but you risk causing damage to your car. And you risk emotional damage by not making deposits.

For each city I visit, I have a list of people I care about, so I contact them when I'm coming to town to schedule time to get together. I also take time each month to go over my list of connections and reconnect and nurture the relationships I feel need to be nurtured.

Relationships need to be nurtured. If a relationship isn't nurtured, the connection will fade. Create a plan of concrete steps to take to nurture your relationships. This may consist of creating and

---

33   Covey, Stephen R. The 7 habits of highly effective people: powerful lessons in personal change. New York: Free Press, 2014.

managing an email list of the people in your life, sending out birthday cards, or scheduling weekly coffee dates. Be intentional and adjust the steps you take to nurture your relationships based on what's working and what's not.

"A dream you dream alone is only a dream. A dream you dream together is reality," John Lennon once said. To make real change as a mental health superhero, creating connections is required, rewarding, and life changing. We thrive off of these connections. Do yourself, and the world, a favor and start creating stronger connections around the shared goal transforming the stigma surrounding mental health and mental wellness.

We're not going to change the entire world overnight. It's going to be incremental. As you positively affect one relationship—it has domino effect that impacts other relationships. Connections are contagious. Start spreading them.

'There is no more neutrality in the world. You either have to be part of the solution, or you're going to be part of the problem.'

— T. Siedner, London NW2

CONCLUSION

Superheroes fight. They understand the importance of what they're fighting for, commit to that cause, and then fight like hell.

And what we're fighting against—Stigma—cowers to those strong enough to confront it. Stigma relies on ignorance and avoidance to grow. When we avoid the topic of mental health, it grows.

This is where you, a superhero in training, comes in. Are you going to join me in Transforming Stigma™, or will you stand on the sidelines and let this problem continue to grow?

I'm asking you. No, I'm begging you, to fight, to take ownership of the solution to the gigantic problem that is the stigma surrounding mental health.

Mental health challenges are a global plague. By becoming a mental wellness superhero and Transforming Stigma™, you have a unique opportunity and power to help yourself, those you love, and billions of people that you will never, ever meet.

The impact that will come from Transforming Stigma™ extends far beyond mental health. Many of the problems that we face in this world are impacted negatively because of mental health challenges and the stigma surrounding them. From poverty, to homelessness, to economies, a mentally healthy world will have a positive impact on each of these.

As I mentioned at the start of this book, each year, approximately 44,000 Americans alone die by suicide. These suicides come at an extremely high price for their friends and family, and even for the country, as the cost of these deaths is $50 billion dollars annually.

A single death by suicide has an enormous effect on the lives of those who were close to the individual and the whole community who realize someone was suffering. Knowing that someone we knew died by suicide naturally makes us think about the battles that we experience internally, and the fear that it could lead to our own death.

One of the reasons I began Transforming Stigma™ was because I truly believe that suicide should not exist, and it can be prevented. I know that if we put in the effort, we can drastically reduce and perhaps eliminate suicide in our world.

Sound impossible? This is why we need your superhero capabilities.

You may think that because you are one person your efforts might not be noticed by anyone, except perhaps those closest to you. But I guarantee that if you apply the ideas in this book, you will see a dramatic change in your own life, the lives of the people you love, and the lives of the people around you.

Ultimately, your efforts will help change the world for the better, for real. This is not a superhero fantasy in a comic book—this is a non-fiction tale of how we can overcome one of the biggest challenges we face in the world today.

What You Can Do Right Now

During your journey through this book, you have been preparing to become a mental wellness superhero. To recap, here's what you need to know:

- The topic of "mental health" refers to thoughts, feelings, and behavior.

- The stigma surrounding this topic is also about thoughts, feelings, and behavior.

- Within stigma:

  - Thoughts are *stereotypes*.

  - Feelings are *prejudice*.

  - Behavior is *discrimination*.

- Whether it's you who is struggling or someone you love, mental health challenges are both confusing and frustrating.

- We are tribal people by nature and nobody wants to be the odd or weird one in the group.

- The Stigma Cycle™: Stigma starts with shame; shame leads to silence; silence leads to sabotage, self-destructive behavior, social injustice, and suicide. This is a never-ending cycle that is experienced by people who live with mental health challenges and people who love someone who is lives with mental health challenges.

- Shame is transformed through being intentional about self-care.

- Silence is transformed through being intentional about having uncomfortable conversations.

- Sabotage, self-destructive behavior, social injustice, and suicide are transformed through being intentional about connecting with others.

The next step of your training—the one and most important step that you can take right now is GO TO THERAPY! Regardless of whether or not you're living with a mental health challenge or not, it's important that you explore your own mental health and are ready and prepared to use your superhero powers to save lives.

Think of therapy as your ongoing training. It will not be easy, but changing the world takes dedication and giving your very best. I can honestly tell you that I would not be the person I am today without therapy. In fact, without therapy, I may not be here at all.

Update on Me

As I finish this book, I am healthy, married to an amazing woman, and traveling the world trying to transform stigma. My mental health remains the most important focus in my life because if I am not mentally healthy, the positive impact I can have on those I serve is limited, if not completely destroyed. Through the many ups and downs I have had over the years, my therapist and the therapy I recieve has been a consistent positive, which is extremely important during the tough times.

On July 29th, 2016, after a long battle with cancer, my mother died. She had a profound impact on my life in positive and negative ways.

I've made it a point to be extra sensitive when it comes to discussing my family and friends in my work as both a writer and speaker. As a rule, I do my best to make sure I minimize any of the negative things I could say about the people I know.

However, after my mother passed, I felt that it was my responsibility to openly discuss my mother and her impact on myself and others—not to hurt her reputation or let my anger out, but to help in my healing process and to raise awareness of how our own thoughts, feelings, and behaviors impact those around us.

Leading up to my mother's death, my therapist played an active role in making sure I got the support that I needed, whether that meant extra sessions or the occasional late-night phone call if I was struggling. As I processed the thoughts and feelings around my mother, before and after her death, I've come to realize that she wasn't emotionally available to me in ways that I needed as a child.

Because of this, I never learned healthy ways to process difficult emotions. The only way I knew how to process them was to act out with anger and aggression, which explains my behavior as a child.

I've also come to realize I misbehaved most in school when the teachers were women. Since a very young age, I've had repressed anger towards women because of my relationship with my mother.

My mother didn't have many close friends, and she clearly had mental health challenges of her own, yet she never sought out help. In the 37 years that I had known her, she never apologized even once for the smallest thing. If she did, it was a fake apology spoken with the intention of shifting any perceived criticism away from her as quickly as possible.

During conversations, she couldn't go more than five minutes without turning the focus to herself. She wasn't able to truly listen to anyone.

Towards the end of her life, I began to become acutely aware of her behavior patterns. I then started setting boundaries, and at times, kept my distance in order to love her while avoiding emotional triggers.

Regardless of the emotional trauma I experienced as a result of my interaction with my mother, I loved my mother. I am beyond grateful for the time, effort, money, and sacrifices that her and my father made for my brother and me. At the same time, I have to acknowledge the emotional trauma that I experienced growing up.

As I continue to work through my mental health challenges, I'm doing much better these days. I see my therapist weekly and have begun seeing a psychiatrist. I'm currently taking medication for depression and anxiety.

In addition to therapy, I regularly attend a support group. The peer support has helped me to take a hard look in the mirror at myself and how I process emotions through listening to others' stories.

In early 2017, I found myself having several mental health breakdowns, and one of them led to spending a night in the psychiatric emergency room of my local hospital. From the breakdowns in 2017, I learned I have spent my entire life running away from difficult feelings.

To stop doing this, my therapist gave me the toughest prescription that anyone has ever given me for my mental health challenges: learn to sit with my feelings.

Sitting with my feelings means that I no longer run away from them. Naturally, we all strive to find what's comfortable to us and never let go, even if it's harmful. I became comfortable with trying to bury my feelings.

My therapist recommended that I instead run towards them. This was the scariest thing I've ever done, but I am now better able to process them in a healthy way. I don't always succeed with trying to embrace and process what I'm going through, but each attempt has been therapeutic and has decreased the impact and intensity of my pain that previously took weeks or months to go away, like a bout of anxiety or depression.

All of these efforts have lead me to strive for a new way of living which is called emotional sobriety. Dr. Ingrid Mathieu, in a Psychology Today blog post, describes emotional sobriety as "less about the quality of the feeling ("good" or "bad") and more about the general ability to feel one's feelings." Dr. Mathieu goes on to explain more about emotional sobriety:

"Sometimes emotional sobriety is about tolerating what you are feeling. It is about staying sober no matter what you are feeling. It means that you don't have to blame yourself or your program because life can be challenging. It means that you don't necessarily need to do something to make the feeling go away. Many people will take their bad feeling and try to pray it, meditate it, service it, spiritually distract themselves from it, thinking that this means they are working a good program." [34]

For me, emotional sobriety is being able to fully embrace whatever it is that I'm feeling at a given moment and approach it with curiosity, which is much easier said than done. If I can better understand what I'm feeling and why, I can then make better decisions and control my emotions and reactions to what happens in my life and inside my mind. It has helped me power up for the continued fight against stigma that you have bravely joined me on.

Congratulations! You are now ready to start your superhero journey. Speaking of journeys, I want to thank you for coming on this one with me. You've made it to the end, and I appreciate the time that you have invested in reading this, and I hope that you have

---

34   Noam Shpancer. "Emotional Acceptance: Why Feeling Good is Bad." September 2010, 8. https://www.psychologytoday.com/blog/insight-therapy/201009/emotional-acceptance-why-feeling-bad-is-good.

gotten something of value from it. If you have found it helpful, I encourage you to share it with someone whom you feel may benefit from it.

This is not just about you. This is not just about me. This is not just about someone you love; this is about the human race. The work you do as a mental wellness superhero, even at the smallest level, will have a profound impact on lives that you will never see.

Now I hope I've given you some tools for change. I hope that you take the willingness to step up to the plate, take that first step of seeking out therapy, and become the mental health superhero that we need you to be.

Thank you for Transforming Stigma™!

Kind regards,

Mike Veny

THANK YOU

Thank you for reading my book, my story, my journey, and my ideas.

Please leave a helpful and honest review on Amazon.com so it can help others struggling with mental health issues, their loved ones, or those to seek to know more about what I have learned.

If you would like to learn more about my products and services, please visit TransformingStigma.com.

Thank you and remember that you are a superhero.

Transforming Stigma™ starts with YOU!

ACKNOWLEDGEMENTS

The completion of this book could have not been made possible without the participation, support, and help from a long list of people. I appreciate all of their efforts and am grateful for their contributions. However, I would like to express sincere appreciation and indebtedness mainly to the following:

I am thankful to Michael Luchies and his gifts as a writer. None of this would have been possible without him. His attention to detail and willingness to disagree with me is what got this book finished.

Special thanks to Jeff Yalden, Brett Francis, and Kevin Hines for their tips and advice. I am grateful for how they're changing lives as mental health speakers and writers.

To Wendy Wood for challenging my thinking around the subject of mental health.

I place on record my sincerest thanks to my mentor, Michael Hartstein, along with my mastermind group consisting of Dr. Isaiah Pickens, Brendan Finnegan, and Dr. Sidney Hankerson. They inspire me, challenge me, and are great role models.

To Bud Clayman, Glenn Holsten, and the rest of the team at OC87 Recovery Diaries, I am grateful that they believed in me and invested so much in me. The work they are doing is having a powerful impact on the world.

I also thank Andrew Lee, Katherine Dirks, Kristina Brooks, and the rest of the team at HealthCentral.com for believing in me and encouraging me to step outside of my comfort zone.

To my brother Jason, my father, and the rest of my family, for loving me despite how much my behavior has harmed them. I hope they find it in their hearts to forgive me and know that I am working hard on a daily basis to take responsibility, stay healthy, and grow. I love my family.

I take this opportunity to thank my mother, Deborah Veny. I think she would have enjoyed reading this book and would have called me to discuss every chapter. I love her, miss her, and hope that her spirit heals as she reincarnates into her next life.

And most importantly, I'd like to thank my wife, Denelle. I am grateful for her unconditional love and support of me.

BOOK MIKE VENY TO SPEAK

"The only way to do great work is to love what you do."

— Steve Jobs

Mike Veny is one of America's leading mental health speakers and a high-energy drum circle facilitator. He delivers educational, engaging, and entertaining presentations to meetings and conferences throughout the world. As a 2017 PM360 ELITE Award Winner, Mike is recognized as one of the 100 most influential people in the healthcare industry. He starred in several OC87 Recovery Diaries documentary films, two of which were featured at the 2017 Reel Minds Film series.

Mike is fiercely committed to wellness, suicide prevention, and helping people work together more smoothly. If you are looking for a proven speaker who can address the stigma surrounding mental health and deliver a corporate drumming event, then you have come to the right place.

With 15 years of experience electrifying audiences and making meeting planners look good, his mission is to empower people to connect authentically.

Mike's path to becoming a public speaker became evident at an early age. **He convinced the staff at psychiatric hospitals to discharge him three times during his childhood.** In addition to being hospitalized as a child, he was expelled from 3 schools, attempted suicide, and was medicated in efforts to reduce his emotional instability and behavioral outbursts. By the fifth grade, Mike was put in a special education class. Aside from getting more individualized attention from the teacher, he learned that pencil erasers make a great sound when tapped on a desk. He had no idea that drumming would become his career or his path to recovery.

Event planners say remarkable things about the impact his work has done for their events.

"Mike Veny has an innate ability to connect with people, draw them out, and get them to participate. This is not an easy task when you are responsible for closing a two and a half day conference on a Friday."

MaryBeth Schneider – Assistant Executive Director for Training and Self-Advocacy, NYSARC

"After more than 10 years of coordinating conference speakers and keynoters, Mike was refreshingly easy to work with and flexible enough to structure his program to deliver exactly what we needed. I would recommend Mike as a keynoter to a wide variety of groups and situations. I don't think you'll be disappointed!"

— Carla H. Falkenstein Pennsylvania Housing Finance Agency

"We had many compliments about your professionalism and the information you presented. Your subject matter, expertise, and the ability to provide the necessary information and resources to the Work/Family representatives were critical to the successful delivery of this important training."

– Maurice Staten from United Auto Workers & Michael V. Coletta from General Motors

Similar benefits await when you hire Mike to take your event to the next level. What sets Mike apart from other speakers is his authenticity and his straightforward, easy-to-understand tools that audience members can apply immediately. It's that simple!

You can feel confident having Mike as your keynote speaker. Over the years, his expertise has been honored with remarkable and notable accolades, including serving on the Board of Directors of The Fender Music Foundation, the Rotary Club of Wall Street New York, an Ambassador for Self Employment in the Arts, and a presenter at the Haiti Entrepreneurship Camp.

Mike's perspectives have been featured on ABC, NBC, and CBS news. He's a writer for Corporate Wellness Magazine and HealthCentral.com. Mental Illness is An Asset, his compelling TEDx talk has been used in college classrooms and gotten sensational reviews.

Five things about him and his experience that might surprise and delight you – while serving your work together:

1. He does not use notes in his presentations.
2. He's a member of the Rotary Club of Wall Street. Being a Rotarian has contributed to his happiness.
3. He loves to travel and is obsessed with luggage, packing techniques, and travel checklists.
4. He takes his morning routine very seriously.
5. He enjoys a really good steak cooked medium rare.

Connect with Mike today and explore how he can add value to your upcoming and give your audience the memory of a lifetime.

TransformingStigma.com

Made in the USA
Columbia, SC
02 May 2019